Dedication

I would like to dedicate this book to my grandmothers, grandfather, my parents, and especially my children and grandchildren. My grandmother, aka Own Mama, used to say opposition builds character and we have a whole family of characters!!!

Here is the list of characters

Own Mama: My mother's mom, also known as Granny. She was born and raised in a family who were a part of the Church of the Brethern, which was an offshoot of the Amish.

Grandpa LeClair: My mother's father, who was also a French chef. Born in Canada or upstate NY; don't know for sure.

Grandma Mary: My dad's mother. She was born into a family that were LDS(Mormon) in Ritchfield, Utah.

Grandpa Leo: My dad's Father: Born in Salt Lake City, Utah.

Mama: Betty Jean LeClair Solomon. My mother, born in Los Angeles, California.

Daddy: Jack Lee Solomon. My father, born in Salt Lake City, Utah.

Me: Linda Lee Solomon Carr, born in Los Angeles, California.

Laurie: My sister, Laurel Lee Solomon Cobb, born in Los Angeles, California.

Jackie: My brother, Jack Lee Solomon Jr., born in Los Angeles, California.

My children: Richard Lee, Kristina Lee, and Jason Lee.

My husband: Richard Lewis Carr: Born at home in LA County.

The reason I listed all my family members is because they are the reason I cook, and I LOVE to cook. I learned to cook from the best teachers in the world, they taught with love and patience. Everyone knows that the Amish cook with everything good and healthy. Who cooks better than the French! Then there are the Mormons, we can make meat out of wheat!!

It all started for me in high school cooking class, we were making pies and my team of classmates were not the best at cooking, let alone making pies. Suffice it to say we failed that assignment. I went home determined to ace this project!! I made nine pies on Saturday and Sunday and there was only one slice left for the teacher on Monday. I got an "A" in that class for the year.

As I graduated from school and got married and had children, I wanted to cook the best for them. Then they started to get food allergies, so I started to find cookbooks with recipes that were healthy and that they liked. Then I became addicted to cookbooks, I now have about 300 of them and counting.

The main reason I started this cookbook 10 years ago, was to put down in writing my favorite recipes all in the same place. Now when I want to find a certain recipe, I don't have to look in 300 cookbooks, I just go to one book, because my memory isn't what it used to be. When I want to take a walk down memory lane or get inspired for ,"What's for dinner," I now just open, "MY COOKBOOK." I also wanted a legacy for my children and grandchildren. I only have three grandsons at the time of this printing, but they all love to cook and it's a great pleasure to help them learn. Because if they know how to cook they will never go hungry, no matter what the ingredients are.

Table of Contents

Salads & Odds & Ends . . . . pg. 5

Soups & Main Dishes . . . . pg. 19

Bread . . . . pg. 55

Cookies . . . . pg. 77

Deserts . . . . pg. 99

Canning . . . . pg. 143

Salads & Odds & Ends

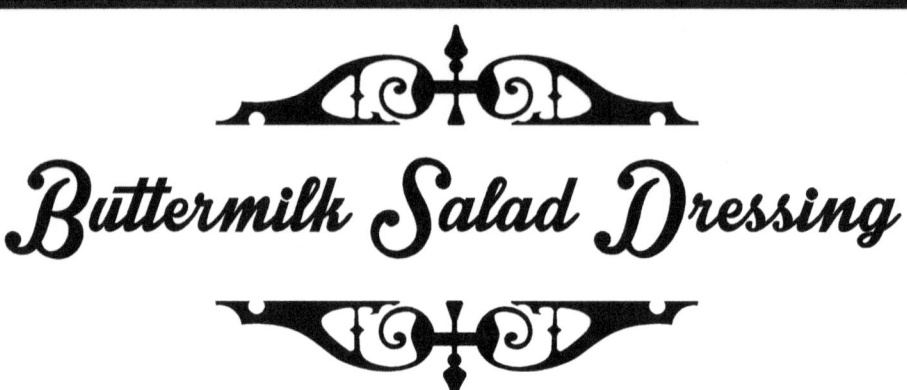

Buttermilk Salad Dressing

½ cup sour cream
1 cup mayonnaise
½ cup buttermilk

1 tsp. seasoned salt*
2 Tbsp. minced fresh parsley
1 Tbsp. minced onion

Mix all the ingredients together and chill until ready to use.

*For seasoned salt, see following page.

Seasoned Salt Mixture

1 cup salt
¼ cup fresh ground black pepper
¼ cup garlic powder
1 Tbsp. onion powder

Mix well and store in an airtight container.

This seasoned salt is good on all kinds of things, like chicken, beef, ribs and so much more.

Thousand Island Salad Dressing

1 cup mayonnaise
¼ cup chili sauce
¼ cup cream
1 Tbsp. onion, minced
1 Tbsp. green pepper, minced

The juice of one lemon
Salt to taste
Pepper to taste
1 grated hard boiled egg
Dash of Worcestershire sauce

Mix all together and chill. This is great!!!

Three Bean Salad

1 can each - cut green beans, kidney beans, cut wax beans
½ cup chopped green pepper
½ cup finely sliced onion

¾ cup sugar
⅔ cup vinegar
⅓ cup vegetable oil

Drain the beans and place in a large bowl. Combine the sugar, vinegar, and the oil. Pour mixture over the beans, peppers, and onions. Add 1 tsp. each of salt and pepper. Toss and chill overnight.

Makes 6 to 8 servings.

Pear Salad

½ cup grape seed oil
2 Tbsp. balsamic vinegar
2 tsp. whole-grain mustard
2 tsp. sugar
1 tsp. sea or kosher salt
Freshly ground pepper
½ cup pecans, lightly toasted and roughly chopped

⅓ cup dried cranberries, or cherries
8 cups chopped salad greens, like kale, romaine, baby spinach, any dark green leafy greens
2 firm but ripe Bosc pears (do not peel). Cut in half and remove the seeds, then slice into cubes.
½ cup feta cheese

In a jar, mix all of the grape seed oil, balsamic vinegar, whole-grain mustard, sugar, salt, and pepper. Put the lid on and shake really well.

Toss all the dressing and remaining ingredients together in a large salad bowl.

This is a GREAT salad all by itself!!!!

This serves 8 and can be doubled.

My Grandma's Chicken Salad

3 cups cooked chicken, chopped
3 ribs celery, sliced
½ cup chopped green olives w/ pimentos
3 hard boiled eggs, sliced

1 head iceberg lettuce, cut up
¼ cup vinegar
1 tsp. garlic salt
1 cup mayonnaise

Mix the vinegar and the garlic salt together in a large bowl. To the bowl add the celery, chopped olives, and chicken, and mix well. Top with the lettuce and keep in the fridge until ready to serve. When ready, mix in the mayonnaise and top with the sliced eggs. This salad serves 6, and I usually serve a nice crusty garlic bread along with it.

Asian Chicken Salad

1 head cabbage, sliced thinly
2 green onions, sliced
½ cup each sesame seeds and
sliced almonds, lightly toasted
2 cups cooked chicken,
cut into bite size pieces

½ cup cilantro, chopped
2 cups fried wonton strips
¾ cup Asian salad dressing
½ of a bell pepper, thinly sliced

On a cookie sheet lined with parchment paper, toast the sesame seeds and sliced almonds in an oven set on broiler. Let cool. Slice the cabbage very thin and place in a large bowl. Add the chicken, chopped green onions, bell pepper, cilantro, toasted sesame seeds, and toasted almonds, then mix. Add the dressing and mix well. Top with the fried wontons and serve. This makes enough for 6 people.

Chinese Salad

1 head cabbage (finely chopped)
5 green onions (chopped)
3 Tbsp. sesame seeds (toasted)
½ cup sliced almonds (toasted)
3 Tbsp. rice wine vinegar
2 ½ Tbsp. sugar
1 package Top Ramen noodles

Mix the cabbage and the green onions together. Toast the sesame seeds and almonds, then mix with the cabbage. Break the ramen noodles into small bits and mix with the cabbage. Mix the rice wine vinegar, sugar, and the Top Ramen seasoning package together, and pour over the salad. Mix well.

Sweet and Sour Sauce

1 cup sugar
½ cup pineapple juice
½ cup vinegar
2 Tbsp. chopped bell pepper

½ tsp. salt
1 Tbsp. cornstarch
2 Tbsp. water

Heat in a saucepan the first five ingredients until boiling, then simmer for 5 minutes. Combine the cornstarch with the water and add to the hot mixture. Cook and stir until the sauce thickens. Cool and store in the refrigerator.

Shrimp with Zesty Cocktail Sauce

¼ cup Old Bay seasoning
3 pounds medium shrimp, peeled and deveined
⅔ cup ketchup
⅓ cup chili sauce

2 Tbsp. prepared horseradish
½ tsp. lemon zest
1 Tbsp. fresh lemon juice
1 tsp. Worcestershire sauce

Bring 3 quarts of water to a boil in a large pot. Stir in Old Bay seasoning and shrimp. Cook for 2 to 3 minutes or until shrimp turn pink. Drain, but do not rinse the seasoning off the shrimp. Put shrimp into bowl and chill in refrigerator. Combine ketchup and the remaining ingredients in a bowl and mix well. Serve with chilled boiled shrimp.

Taco Seasonings

2 tsp. garlic salt
1 tsp. season salt
1 Tbsp. ground cumin

1 Tbsp. ground chili powder
1 Tbsp. dried onion flakes

In a small bowl mix all the ingredients together.

Add to one pound of ground beef in a frying pan, and you have meat for great tacos!

Cereal Party Mix

3 cups Chex corn cereal
3 cups Chex rice cereal
3 cups Chex wheat cereal
1 cup salted peanuts
1 cup pretzel sticks
1 cube of butter

2 Tbsp. Worcestershire sauce
1 ½ tsp. seasoned salt
1 tsp. garlic powder
½ tsp. onion powder

Preheat oven to 250°F. In a large baking pan add all the cereal, nuts, and the pretzels, and mix together. In a small saucepan, or microwaveable dish, add the Worcestershire sauce, butter, seasoned salt, garlic powder, and the onion powder, then heat until the butter melts. Stir until well blended and pour over the cereal mixture. Mix all together and bake in oven for 1 hour, mixing every 15 minutes.

My grandma Mary would make this for her bridge club every Christmas, and every time I make it I think of her.

Beef Jerky

1 ½ to 2 lbs. flank steak, frozen but thawed slightly
⅔ cup soy sauce
⅔ cup Worcestershire sauce
2 Tbsp. sugar
2 tsp. freshly ground pepper
2 tsp. onion powder
1 tsp. liquid smoke
½ tsp. pepper flakes

Slice the steak with the grain, into very thin, long strips. In a zip lock gallon size bag, add all the other ingredients then the meat. Close up the bag and mix everything together very well. Place the bag in the refrigerator for 3 to 6 hours, or up to one day, turning the bag often.

Remove the meat strips from the bag and place on a cookie rack on top of a cookie sheet, lined with parchment paper.

Put into an oven set at the lowest possible temperature setting. Mine will only go to 200°F, so I keep the oven door open slightly with a wooden spoon.

Let dry for about 4 hours, checking often. You don't want the jerky to get to stiff and dried out.

Store in a zip lock bag in the refrigerator.

Soups & Main Dishes

Sausage Lentil Soup

1 ¼ cups dry lentils, rinsed
1 ½ pounds Polish sausage, sliced
1 6-ounce can tomato paste
3 potatoes, peeled and cubed
1 medium onion, chopped

1 cup chopped carrots
1 cup chopped celery
1 ½ tsp. instant beef bouillon granules
¾ tsp. dried thyme, crushed
⅛ tsp. pepper

In a pan combine lentils and 5 cups water; bring to a boil. Reduce heat. Cover and simmer for 30 minutes. In an electric slow cooker combine undrained lentils with the remaining ingredients. Cover and cook on low heat for 6 hours.

Makes 6 servings

This was Kristina's favorite soup and was what she wanted for her 16th birthday dinner.

Barbecued Chili Beans

1 lb. ground beef
6 slices bacon, chopped
1 Tbsp. chopped garlic
1 Tbsp. chili powder
2 cans of chilies
2 tsp. cumin

1 tsp. salt
1 tsp. ground black pepper
½ cup BBQ sauce
3 cans pinto beans
1 large can tomato sauce

In a large saucepan brown the ground beef and bacon. Add the rest of the ingredients and simmer for a couple of hours.

Fresh Tomato Soup

¼ cup butter
1 red onion, finely chopped
1 small carrot, finely chopped
4 lb. ripe tomatoes, peeled
and coarsely chopped

3 cups chicken stock
1 fresh basil sprig
1 ½ cup fresh bread crumbs
1 cup cream
Salt and pepper to taste

In a large saucepan, melt the butter over medium heat. Add the onion and carrot and sauté until translucent. Add the tomatoes, stock, and basil. Bring to a boil, reduce the heat and cover and simmer for about 30 minutes. Add the bread crumbs and in small batches, put the soup through a food mill.

Add the soup in small batches into a blender and blend until creamy. Pour all the soup back into the saucepan and add the cream. Add the salt and pepper to taste, reheat and enjoy.

This is a great way to use up all those tomatoes in the garden, and it freezes great.

Ham and Bean Soup

1 ham bone or smoked shank
2 cups great northern white beans
10 cups water
2 cups chopped celery
1 large onion, chopped

1 bay leaf
1 tsp. ground pepper
1 tsp. Worcestershire sauce
3 Tbsp. chopped parsley
2 tsp. salt or to taste

Wash and pick through the beans for bad ones or small rocks. Put the beans in a large soup pot with the ham bone and cover with the water. Add the rest of the ingredients, except the salt, and bring the water to a boil. Lower the heat and simmer 4 to 5 hours, with the lid on, or until the beans are soft and tender. When the beans are ready then add the salt. Just before serving remove the ham bone and pick the meat off the bone and add it to the soup. Discard the bones.

If you add salt to the beans before they are cooked thoroughly they will not get soft.

This will serve 8-10.

If you have ham for, lets say, Christmas or Easter, or just any time, and you don't want to make soup just then, freeze it until you are ready.

My grandmother would make this soup in the winter and it would warm the house and the tummy.

Creamy Pumpkin Soup

2 Tbsp. butter
1 medium onion, finely chopped
4 cups peeled, chopped pumpkin meat or canned pumpkin (unsweetened)
1 large potato, diced
2 medium tomatoes, peeled, seeded, and chopped
4 cups chicken stock or water

1 tsp. salt
½ tsp. sepper
1 cup chopped celery leaves
2 Tbsp. chopped parsley
2 Tbsp. butter
½ cup heavy cream
Croutons

In a soup pot melt the butter and cook the onion until it is tender. Add the vegetables and the stock. Season with the salt and pepper. Add the celery leaves, and the fresh parsley to taste. Cook the vegetables until they are tender. Puree the mixture in a food mill, blender, or food processor. Rinse the pot and return the soup to it. Add the butter and cream, as desired, and heat the soup through. Serve the soup with croutons.

Serves 6.

Cauliflower Soup

1 small head cauliflower,
  cut into flowerettes
4 large potatoes, peeled, and cubed
½ cup celery, chopped
½ cup onion, chopped

5 cups milk
1 tsp. salt
Freshly ground pepper
2 Tbsp. butter
1 cup heavy cream
Chopped parsley

Put the cauliflower, potatoes, celery, onions, milk, and salt in a large saucepan. Add pepper to taste. Bring the mixture to a boil and simmer it, covered, for 30 minutes, or until the vegetables are tender. Puree the mixture in a food mill, blender, or a food processor. Rinse the pot and return the soup to it, and stir in the cream and the butter over low heat. Serve the soup in warmed bowls and sprinkle with the parsley.

Serves 8.

Zucchini Casserole

1 ½ lbs. zucchini squash. About 6 medium with ends trimmed.
¼ cup chopped onion
1 egg, beaten
¼ cup butter
1 ½ tsp. sugar
½ tsp. salt
½ tsp. pepper
¼ cup bread crumbs

Preheat oven to 375°F.

Grease a 2-quart casserole dish. Cut the zucchini into one inch pieces and boil until tender, then drain and mash. Add the onion, egg, 2 Tbsp. of the butter, the salt, sugar, and the pepper. Place the squash mixture into the prepared casserole dish and smooth the top. Melt the remaining butter and pour all over the top. Sprinkle with the bread crumbs. Bake for 30 minutes, or until lightly browned.

Serves 6 to 8.

Sausage & Rice Casserole

1 can chicken and rice soup
2 cups celery - sliced into small pieces
½ medium onion, chopped
1 lb. Sausage

1 cup rice, uncooked
1 can of water
1 tsp. salt
½ tsp. pepper

In a skillet sauté the sausage, celery, and the onion until sausage is cooked. Add the salt and pepper. In a 2 quart casserole dish with a lid, mix the soup with the rice and water. Add the sausage mixture to the casserole dish with the rice mixture and blend. Bake in a 375°F oven for about one and a half hours, or until the rice is tender.

Serves 6.

This dish is one of my father's favorites, and was served at my wedding rehearsal dinner. It can be made in large batches in a much bigger casserole dish.

I think the recipe came from my grandma Mary, and I think she got it from the church relief society.

Sauerbraten

4-5 pound beef chuck pot roast
1 ½ cups red wine vinegar
2 chopped onion
1 rib celery, chopped
1 carrot, chopped
½ cup red wine

8 whole pepper corns
4 whole allspice
4 cloves
2 bay leaves
½ cup crushed ginger snaps

Mix all, except the meat, in a saucepan and bring to a boil for 5 minutes. Let cool. Pour liquid into a locking plastic bag and add the meat. Close the bag and refrigerate for 3 or 4 days.

Remove the meat from the bag and brown in a skillet with just a little vegetable oil. Brown meat very well on all sides. Put meat in a stewing pot. Strain juices and pour over the meat. Chop and add fresh carrots, celery, and onions. Simmer on medium heat for 3 hours. Remove meat from pot and in a blender blend the juices and the vegetables. Pour the blended juices back into the pot and thicken with ½ cup crushed ginger snaps to make a gravy. Slice the meat and serve with the gravy.

Italian Beef Rolls
(Braciole)

4 ¾ pounds beef top round steaks, each cut about ¼ inch thick
1 pound sweet Italian sausage links
2 cups lightly packed celery leaves
2 white bread slices, crumbled
⅓ cup olive oil
1 large onion, diced
2 large garlic cloves, minced
4 large carrots, cut into 2" by ½" strips
1 16 oz. can tomato puree
1 14 ½ oz. can beef broth
½ cup dry red wine
1 Tbsp. brown sugar
2 tsp. salt
½ tsp. pepper
2 16 oz. packages spaghetti

On cutting board, with a meat mallet or dull edge of a French knife, pound each steak to about ⅛ inch thick. Overlap long edges of two steaks to make one large one. Pound overlap as flat as possible. Remove casings from sausage links. Spread steaks with thin layer of half of the sausages. Top with half of the celery leaves and half of the bread crumbs. Starting at the narrow end, roll steaks, jelly-roll fashion, and tie securely with string. Repeat with remaining steaks, sausage, celery leaves and bread crumbs.

In an 6 to 8 quart Dutch oven over medium-high heat, in hot olive oil, cook steak rolls until well browned on all sides; remove from Dutch oven to a large platter, and set aside.

Using remaining oil in the Dutch oven, cook onion, garlic and carrots 5 minutes. Stir in tomato puree, broth, red wine, brown sugar, salt, and pepper. Return the steak rolls to the Dutch oven; heat to boiling. Reduce heat to low; cover and simmer 1 ½ hours or until steak rolls are fork-tender.

During the last 30 minutes the steak rolls are cooking, cook spaghetti as the label directs. Drain and place in a warm large bowl.

Remove rolls to cutting board; remove strings; cut rolls crosswise into ½ inch thick slices; arrange on a warm platter. Pour some sauce over slices and serve with remainder in a gravy boat with spaghetti.

Makes 12 servings.

Fried Fish with Beer Batter Coating

½ cup beer
½ cup water
½ tsp. salt
½ tsp. pepper

1 tsp. minced garlic
¾ cup flour
¼ cup cornstarch
8 Fish Fillets

Combine all the ingredients, except the fish fillets, and beat well with a whisk. Fill a deep pan with vegetable oil, about ¼ to ½ inch deep. Heat oil to 375°F. Pat the fish dry and coat thoroughly with the batter. Drop the fish into the hot oil with tongs and cook until golden brown; about 10 to 15 minutes.

Serve with malt vinegar or tartar sauce.

Serves 4.

Macaroni and Cheese

10 oz. elbow macaroni
2 cups shredded cheese, this could be any kind of cheese you like.
2 Tbsp. butter
1 Tbsp. flour
2 cups milk
Salt and pepper to taste
1 Tbsp. onion, finely chopped

Cook the macaroni in plenty of boiling salted water, the water should taste like sea water, until al dente-about 15 minutes. In a large saucepan, melt the butter and add the onion and cook until the onion is soft. Add the flour and then the milk and bring them to a boil. Stir with a wire whisk until thick and creamy. Add the cheese and whisk until well combined. Add to the cheese mixture to the macaroni and combine. Pour into a large baking dish and bake for 30 minutes in a 350°F. oven.

Puttanesca

3 large garlic cloves, pressed through a garlic press
1 can stewed Italian tomatoes with oregano and basil
¼ cup good olive oil

2 Tbsp. capers, rinsed and chopped
½ cup black olives, coarsely chopped
½ pound of angle hair pasta
Salt to taste

Bring a large pot of salted water to boil. In the mean time, in a large skillet heat the olive oil and add the pressed garlic. Add the capers, black olives and can of stewed tomatoes. Cover and let simmer. Add the pasta to the boiling water and bring the water back to boiling. Cover and turn off the heat, let sit for 11 minutes. Strain the pasta, add to the tomato sauce, and serve with french bread.

Serves 4-6.

Chicken Piccata

2 boneless, skinless chicken breasts, cut in half and pounded into cutlets
Salt and black pepper
All-purpose flour
2 Tbsp. olive oil
½ cup dry white wine

½ cup chicken broth
2 Tbsp. fresh lemon juice
1 Tbsp. drained capers
2 Tbsp. butter
2 Tbsp. chopped parsley

Season the cutlets with salt and pepper, then dredge them in flour. Coat frying pan with olive oil. And heat over medium-high.

Sauté cutlets 2-3 minutes on one side. Flip cutlets over and sauté the other side 1-2 minutes. Transfer cutlets to a warm plate; pour off the fat from the pan.

Deglaze pan with the wine and chicken broth, add the garlic and cook until slightly brown and the liquid is nearly evaporated, about 2 minutes.

Add the lemon juice and the capers. Return the cutlets to the pan and cook on each side for 1 minute. Transfer cutlets to warm plates.

Finish sauce with butter and parsley. Once the butter melts pour sauce over the cutlets, and serve.

Salisbury Steak

1 ½ pounds ground beef
½ cup seasoned bread crumbs
4 Tbsp. ketchup
1 tsp. salt
1 tsp. ground pepper
2 tsp. dry mustard
1 Tbsp. Worcestershire sauce

1 beef bouillon cube, crushed up
1 onion, sliced

Sauce:
2 cups canned beef broth
2 Tbsp. butter
2 Tbsp. olive oil
½ cup red wine
2 Tbsp. cornstarch

Mix the ground beef, seasoned bread crumbs, ketchup, salt, pepper, dry mustard, Worcestershire sauce, and the crushed up bouillon cube, in a big bowl until thoroughly combined. Divide the meat mixture into 6 oblong patties and chill in the fridge for about 1 hour.

When you are ready, put the oil and the butter in a frying pan and heat until pretty hot, add the patties and cook until nice and brown on both sides. Remove them from the pan and pour off all but about 2 Tbsp. of the fat. Add the onions and sauté until tender.

Sauce:
Add the beef broth, reserving ½ cup, the wine, 2 Tbsp. more ketchup, and a dash more of the Worcestershire sauce. With the reserved beef broth, add the cornstarch and mix well then add to the pan and stir until it thickens. Add the patties back to the pan with the sauce, cover, and simmer for about 30 minutes. Serve with mashed potatoes.

Serves 6.

Chicken Parmesan with Fettuccini Alfredo

1 lb. boned chicken breast
¼ cup bread crumbs
½ tsp. salt
⅛ tsp. ground pepper
1 beaten egg

¼ cup parmesan cheese
½ tsp. oregano
½ cup white wine
½ cup olive oil

Chicken Parmesan:

Pound chicken until thin. Pat dry, and cut into serving sized pieces. Combine bread crumbs, parmesan cheese, spices and salt. Set aside.

Beat the eggs in a shallow baking dish, dip the chicken into egg, then crumb mixture, coating both sides. Heat oil in a skillet. Sauté chicken until brown—about 3 minutes for each side. Remove to a warm platter.

Drain off fat, stir in wine and scrape up bits in the skillet until it starts to boil. Pour over the chicken.

Fettuccine Alfredo:

1 package fresh fettuccini noodles
½ cup parmesan cheese
¼ cup butter
¼ cup cream

1 tsp. chopped parsley
¼ tsp. salt
Pepper to taste

Cook pasta according to package instructions. Meanwhile in a pot, melt butter and pour in cream. Add the cheese, parsley, pepper, salt and mix until smooth and creamy. Then stir in noodles.

Makes about 4 servings.

Chicken Enchilada Casserole

2 cups cooked cut up chicken
2 cans (10 oz.) green chili enchilada sauce
1 4 oz. can chopped green chilies
1 can cream of mushroom soup
2 cups sour cream

1 dozen corn tortillas
3 cups grated cheese (cheddar or jack or both work really well)
5 green onions, chopped

Mix the soup, sour cream, and the green chilies together and set aside. Cut the tortillas in half and lay flat in a 7"x12" baking dish, with the flat side around the edge of the dish and down the middle of the dish. Using three tortillas for the first layer, top with the sour cream soup mixture layer first, then the chicken, then the green onions, then the cheese, and lastly the green enchilada sauce. Repeat the layers 2 more times and bake in a 350°F oven for 1 hour.

Serves 6-8.

Orange Chicken

2 eggs
1 ½ tsp. white pepper
1 ½ tsp. salt
3 chicken breast, cut into small chunks
½ cup cornstarch
½ cup flour
4 cups oil, or a deep fryer
2 tsp. chopped garlic

1 Tbsp. grated ginger
½ tsp. red pepper flakes
1 Tbsp. rice wine vinegar
1 ½ Tbsp. soy sauce
5 Tbsp. white vinegar
½ cup orange marmalade
2 Tbsp. cornstarch
4 Tbsp. water

Heat the cooking oil in a deep sided pan or the deep fryer to 350°F.

In a medium sized bowl mix the flour and cornstarch, set aside. In another medium sized bowl scramble the eggs and add the salt and pepper and mix well, set aside. Take the cut up chicken and first dredge it in the egg mixture, then the flour mixture. Then add, a few at a time, the floured chicken pieces to the deep fryer, cook until a golden brown. Remove the chicken and place on a paper towel lined baking sheet, and continue until all the chicken is cooked.

Next in a large frying pan add the garlic, ginger, red pepper flakes, rice wine vinegar, soy sauce, white wine vinegar, and the marmalade and mix and cook until thick and bubbly. Add the chicken to the frying pan and the sauce. Mix the cornstarch with the water and add to the chicken mixture stirring until the sauce is thick and shiny. Serve with rice.

Chicken Pesto Pasta

¼ cup olive oil
2 chicken breast, cut into ½" pieces
4 garlic cloves, finely chopped
¾ cup heavy cream
1 ½ tsp. each of salt and pepper

½ cup grated parmesan cheese
¼ cup pesto
1 can chopped stewed tomatoes, drained
3 cups penne pasta

In a large pot, cook the pasta according to directions on package. Meanwhile in a large frying pan heat olive oil on high heat, place the cut up chicken in the hot oil and sauté until lightly browned. Add the garlic, salt, pepper, and mix well. Remove from pan and set aside. Add the parmesan, cream, pesto, and the tomatoes to the frying pan and mix well. Add back the chicken and mix to heat up, then cover with sauce. Now add the drained pasta, mix well, and eat. Yummy!!!

Makes 4 servings.

Coconut Chicken Curry

Tomatoes, peeled and chopped
2 boneless, skinless, chicken breasts, cut into little pieces
1 red bell pepper, sliced
2 garlic cloves, chopped
2 cups coconut milk
2 cups water

2 carrots, sliced
1 Tbsp. coconut oil
1 tsp. chicken bouillon
½ cumin, ground
¼ tsp. pepper flakes
2 ½ Tbsp. curry powder
1 tsp. paprika

In a large frying pan heat the coconut oil. Add to the medium-hot oil, the onion, garlic, and the rest of the spices and cook for one minute. Add the tomatoes, cooking and stirring until some of the liquid has evaporated. Add the coconut milk, water, and chicken bouillon. Cook, stirring for 3 minutes. Add the carrots, bell pepper, and chicken. Simmer for 3 minutes or until the chicken is cooked through. Serve over rice.

Fried Rice My Way

4 cups cold, cooked rice
4 slices bacon, sliced into small pieces
1 cup green onion, sliced

2 eggs, beaten
2 Tbsp. sesame oil
¼ cup soy sauce

In a large frying pan, on medium heat, cook the bacon until browned, remove to a paper lined plate and set aside. Scrape the bottom of the frying pan and add the cold cooked rice, and cook in the remaining bacon drippings until the rice is hot. Add the sesame oil and the soy sauce stirring until well coated. Add the beaten eggs and stir until well mixed, add the green onions and the bacon and stir to mix them in. It's ready to eat.

Makes 4-6 servings.

Shepherd's Pie

1 lb. ground beef
3 Tbsp. olive oil
½ cup carrots, finely chopped
1 Tbsp. garlic, chopped

1 large clove of garlic
½ cup bell pepper, chopped
½ cup onion, chopped
Salt and pepper to taste

In a large frying pan, over medium to high heat, add the oil and the ground beef and cook until the meat is brown. Add the carrots, onion, bell pepper, garlic, salt, and pepper. Cook the meat mixture until the vegetables are tender, then layer the meat into a baking dish. Set this aside. You can use leftover mashed potatoes or make more mashed potatoes.

Mashed Potatoes

3 large potatoes, peeled and cut into squares
1 large clove of garlic, peeled
6 cups water
½ cup cream
¾ cup parmesan cheese, grated
Salt and pepper to taste
¼ cup butter

Preheat oven to 350°F.

In a large saucepan add the 6 cups of water and bring it to a boil. Add the potatoes and garlic and cook until the potatoes are tender. Drain the water and mash the potatoes adding the butter, salt, and pepper. Stir in the cream and add the parmesan cheese. Top the meat mixture with the mashed potatoes making sure the potatoes cover the meat. Sprinkle the top with a little more cheese and bake in a 350°F oven for 45 minutes.

Serves 6.

Double Stuffed Potatoes

6 potatoes, washed and covered with vegetable oil
1 cup butter, (2 cubes)
1 ½ cups milk, warmed
1 Tbsp. salt
1 tsp. ground pepper
¾ cup sour cream
2 cups shredded cheese, cheddar or jack
3 green onions, chopped

Bake the washed and oiled potatoes on a cookie sheet in a 375°F oven for 1 hour, or until done. When the potatoes are cooked cut in half and scoop out the flesh into a large bowl and mash with a potato masher. Add the butter, salt, and pepper and mix well. To this add the milk, sour cream, and cheese and mix again. Scoop the mixture back into the potato skin shells.

Now, in my family some don't like the green onions, so I fill the cheese potatoes first. Then I mix in the green onions and finish the rest of the potato skins. Now place them all on a cookie sheet and bake them again for about 45 minutes in a 375°F oven. You can make the stuffed potatoes for up to four days ahead of time, keeping them in the fridge until you want to bake them.

Easy Scalloped Potatoes

1 large pkg. frozen hash brown potatoes
½ cup melted butter
2 cups sour cream
1 can cream of mushroom soup
2 cups grated cheese
¼ cup grated onion
2 tsp. salt
½ tsp. pepper

Mix the sour cream, mushroom soup, onions, and the melted butter together. In a baking dish, add a layer of the potatoes then a layer of the sour cream mixture and repeat. End with the top layer consisting of the grated cheese. Bake at 350°F. for about 1 hour.

Serves 8.

Risotto

3 cups chicken stock
2 cups water
½ tsp. saffron or turmeric
2 Tbsp. olive oil
2 Tbsp. butter
1 medium onion, chopped fine

1 ½ cups Arborio rice
1 cup white wine
½ cup grated parmesan cheese
½ tsp. salt
½ tsp. ground pepper

Combine the broth, water, and the saffron in a saucepan and bring to a boil. Turn down the heat to simmer and keep the broth mixture very warm. In a large frying pan, heat the oil and butter. Add the rice and stir to coat. Stir in the wine and bring to a boil; reduce the heat. Add the broth mixture 1 cup at a time, stirring constantly, until the liquid evaporates. Keep adding the broth mixture and stirring and evaporating until all the liquid is incorporated and the rice is creamy and tender. This should take about 15 to 20 minutes. Stir in the parmesan cheese, salt, and pepper. Serve right away.

This makes 8 side dish servings.

Crock Pot Chili Beans

2 lbs. ground beef
4 cloves garlic, finely chopped
3 Tbsp. cooking oil
1 10 oz. can beef broth
1 ½ cups water
2 tsp. sugar
2 tsp. ground cumin
½ tsp. salt

2 bay leaves
1 4 oz. can green chilies chopped
1 Tbsp. ground chili powder
2 Tbsp. dried onion flakes
1 15 oz. can tomato sauce
2 15 oz. can pinto beans
½ cup cornmeal

In a large skillet brown the ground beef in the oil. Add the browned meat and all the ingredients into a crock pot and mix well. Let this all cook on low for 6 hours. When the cooking is all done add the ½ cup of cornmeal and stir until thickened.

Brayden's Amazing Meatballs

1 lb. ground hamburger
1 egg
¼ cup bread crumbs
1 tsp. Italian seasoning
2 tsp. dried onion flakes

½ tsp. celery salt
1 Tbsp. ketchup
¼ tsp. garlic powder
1 tsp. seasoned salt

In a large bowl mix all of the ingredients together and form into golf ball sized meat balls.

In a large sized frying pan heat 2 Tbsp. of cooking oil and 2 Tbsp. of butter. Place the meatballs in the frying pan and cook, on medium heat, until internal temperature is 165°F. Serve and enjoy.

Marinade For Turkey or Chicken

1 cup Dijon mustard
1 cup olive oil
¾ cup lemon juice
½ cup soy sauce
2 garlic cloves, minced

3 sprigs of fresh rosemary, chopped
3 sprigs of fresh thyme, chopped
¼ cup of fresh sage leaves, chopped
¼ cup of fresh oregano, chopped

In a 1 ½ quart bowl, whisk the ingredients until well blended. Place the bird into a large ziplock bag and pour in marinade. For overly large birds, a new trash bag can be used with the opening tied tightly closed. Refrigerate and let marinate for 8 to 24 hours before cooking.

Makes about 3 ½ cups of marinade.

I've been cooking Thanksgiving turkey this way for 30 years and it always comes out great.

Chicken & Noodles

1 chicken, cut up
2 medium onions, chopped
2 large carrots, chopped
2 ribs of celery, chopped

1 tsp. salt
½ tsp. pepper
3 ½ quarts of water
1 recipe homemade noodles*

Place the chicken in a large pot with all the rest of the ingredients, save the noodles. The water should cover the chicken completely. Cover and bring to a boil over high heat; then skim off froth as it forms on the top. Reduce heat and simmer for about 2 hours. Remove the chicken from the pot, allow to cool a bit, then remove the meat from the bones. Discard the skin and bones, and return the meat to the pot. Add the noodles and simmer for about 10 minutes.

*See following page.

Homemade Noodles

1 cup all-purpose flour
¾ tsp. salt
1 egg
1 Tbsp. vegetable oil
3 Tbsp. water

Place the flour in a medium sized mixing bowl. Make a well in the center of the flour, and add the rest of the ingredients. With a fork, stir to combine until a ball of dough forms. Turn dough out onto a lightly floured board and knead until a smooth dough is achieved, about five minutes. Cover dough and allow to rest for 45 minutes. Cut dough in half. Roll out one-half of the dough on a lightly floured board to about 14" x 8" rectangle. Sprinkle dough surface lightly with a bit more flour, flip over, and sprinkle more flour on the other side. Do the same with the other half of the dough. Allow the dough to dry 20 minutes. Roll dough up like a jelly- roll, starting with short side. Using a very sharp knife, cut noodles to the width you prefer. Unroll each slice onto a tea towel, sprinkle with a bit more flour, and allow to stand until the noodles are completely dry, this may take several hours, depending on the humidity in the air.

You can also mix the dough in a food-processor, it works great and saves time.

Hot Chicken Salad

4 cups cooked chicken, chopped into big chunks
2 cups chopped celery
2 Tbsp. chopped onions
⅔ cup toasted almonds
½ a green pepper, chopped
1 small bag of potato chips, crushed, separated into two piles.

2 Tbsp. lemon juice
4 hard boiled eggs, chopped
½ tsp. salt
1 cup shredded cheddar cheese
1 ½ cups mayonnaise

Mix all the ingredients together, except one pile of the potato chips and cheddar cheese, and put into a 9" x 13" baking dish. Top with the second half of the potato chips and bake in a 400°F. oven for 30 minutes. Remove from oven and top with the cheddar cheese and bake another ten minutes.

This is "Big" Richard's favorite dinner. He will eat it until there isn't any left. This is *not* a fat free dinner...I don't fix it very often.

Bread

Old Fashioned Cinnamon Rolls

½ cup sugar
½ tsp. salt
1 package active dry yeast
4 cups all-purpose flour
1 cup milk
¼ cup butter
1 egg

½ cup packed brown sugar
½ cup walnuts, chopped
½ cup raisins
1 ½ tsp. ground cinnamon
¼ cup melted butter
4 tsp. water
1 cup confectioners sugar

In a bowl, combine sugar, salt, yeast, and 1 cup flour. In a saucepan heat milk and ¼ cup butter until warm (120°F to 130°F.) With mixer at low speed, beat liquid into dry ingredients. At medium speed beat 2 minutes. Beat in egg and 1 cup flour; beat 2 minutes. Stir in 1 ½ cups flour.

On a floured board, or a mixer fitted with a dough hook, knead dough until smooth, about 10 minutes. Add in more flour (about ½ cup) while kneading, if necessary. Shape dough into a ball and place in a greased bowl, turning dough over so the top and bottom are greased. Cover and let rise in a warm place away from a draft until doubled, about one hour.

Punch dough down and turn onto a floured surface; cover and let rest 15 minutes. Meanwhile, combine brown sugar, walnuts, raisins, and cinnamon. Grease a 13" by 9" baking pan. Melt ¼ cup butter. On a floured surface roll dough into a 18" by 12" rectangle and brush with melted butter; sprinkle with sugar mixture. Starting with the long side roll dough jelly-roll fashion; pinch seam to seal. With seam-side down, cut roll crosswise into 18 slices; place in the pan, cut side down. Cover and let rise until doubled, about 40 minutes.

Preheat oven to 400°.

Bake for 20 minutes; cool slightly; brush with sugar glaze. Makes 18 rolls.

SUGAR GLAZE: In a small bowl, stir 1 cup confectioners sugar and 4 tsp. water until smooth.

Blueberry Muffins

1 ¾ cup all-purpose flour
½ cup sugar
2 ½ tsp. baking powder
¾ tsp. salt

1 egg
¾ cup milk
⅓ cup vegetable oil
1 cup fresh or frozen blueberries

Preheat oven to 375°F.

Line a 12-muffin, muffin pan with paper liner cups. Sift together the flour, sugar, salt and the baking powder in a medium sized bowl until combined. Add the liquid ingredients all at once to the dry and stir until just mixed. Gently fold in the blueberries.

Divide the batter evenly among the muffin cups, filling each two-thirds full. Bake in preheated oven 25 minutes or until a cake tester comes out clean. Remove muffins to a wire rack to cool slightly. Serve warm or at room temperature.

"A Bucket" of Bran Muffins

2 cups boiling water
1 cup shortening
2 cups 100% bran flakes
4 cups bran buds
2 ½ cups sugar

4 eggs
1 quart buttermilk
5 cups all-purpose flour
4 tsp. baking soda
1 ½ tsp. salt

In a 4 cup measuring cup, or a medium sized bowl, mix the boiling water and the shortening together until the shortening is completely dissolved. Set aside.

Into a large mixing bowl add bran flakes, bran buds, sugar, flour, baking soda, and the salt. Mix well. Break the eggs into a two cup measuring cup, or small bowl, and scramble lightly. In the large bowl of flour and cereal mixture, add the eggs, buttermilk, and water/shortening mixture. Mix very well. At this time you can add any raisins, cranberries, fresh blueberries, (optional), and fold into the batter. Cover and refrigerate for a couple of hours, or overnight.

Grease a muffin tin with baking spray or cupcake papers. Fill each cup with a large ice cream scoop worth of batter and bake in a 400°F oven for 20 minutes.

Store any left over batter in the refrigerator until ready to use. This batter keeps well in the refrigerator for up to two weeks.

Makes 4 to 6 dozen muffins.

Focaccia

1 package (2 ¼ tsp.) quick rise yeast
1 ¼ cups lukewarm water
2 Tbsp. olive oil, plus more for top of loaf
2 tsp. salt
3-3 ½ cups flour
Coarse salt for top of loaf
1 Tbsp. finely chopped rosemary
2 tsp. garlic salt

In a large bowl or the bowl of an electric stand mixer, dissolve the yeast into the lukewarm water. Stir in the olive oil and the salt. Gradually stir in the 3 cups of flour to make a soft dough.

Knead by hand or put the dough hook of the mixer onit, and knead for 10 minutes until the dough pulls away from the side of the bowl, adding a little flour as needed. Add the rosemary and the garlic and mix until it is mixed all the way through.

Form into a ball and place in a greased bowl, turning so all sides are greased. Cover with plastic wrap and let rise in a warm place until doubled in size, about 1 hour.

Grease an 11x17 inch baking sheet with 1 inch sides with olive oil. Turn out dough on to a lightly floured work surface and press flat. Form into a ball. Place on the prepared baking sheet and let rest for 5 minutes. Using your fingers, stretch out the dough so that it evenly covers the pan bottom. Cover with a cloth towel and let rise until puffy, about 30 minutes. Preheat the oven to 400°F.

Uncover the dough and, using your fingertips, make a pattern of dimples at 2 inch intervals over the entire surface. Brush with olive oil and sprinkle with coarse salt.

Bake until golden brown, 15-20 minutes. Cut into pieces and serve warm or cold and sliced sideways for sandwiches.

Pizza Dough

Olive oil
2 ½-3 cups unbleached bread flour
1 ½ tsp. quick-rise yeast
1 ½ tsp. salt
1 cup lukewarm water (110°F)

To make the dough, lightly grease a mixing bowl with a little olive oil. In a food processor fitted with a metal blade, combine 2 ½ cups of the flour, the yeast, and the salt. Pulse briefly to combine. With the motor running, pour in the lukewarm water and process until the mixture clings together, about 25 seconds. If it is too wet, add as much of the remaining flour, ¼ cup at a time, as needed to form a mass. Turn out the dough onto a lightly floured work surface and gather it into a loose ball. Place it in the greased bowl and turn the dough to grease all sides. Cover with plastic wrap and let rise in a warm place until doubled, 35-45 minutes.

Turn dough out onto a lightly floured surface and press flat. Cut in half and form each half into a ball. Let rest for about 5 minutes. Using a rolling pin, roll out each ball into a 12-inch round, making the edges a little thicker than the center. Lay each round on a prepared pizza pan, cover lightly with a cloth and let rise until puffy, 15-20 minutes.

Top with your favorite toppings and bake in a 400°F oven for 20-25 minutes or until the crust is golden and crispy.

Makes two 12-inch pizzas.

White Bread

2 cups milk
1 package active dry yeast
3 Tbsp. sugar
¼ cup (½ stick) butter
1 tsp. salt

4-5 cups unsifted all-purpose flour
1 large egg
1 Tbsp. water
1 tsp. sesame seeds

In a small saucepan, heat milk until bubbles form around side of the pan. Remove ½ cup of milk to a small bowl. Set aside to cool to between 110°F and 115°F, then stir in yeast and 1 Tbsp. sugar. Let mixture stand until foamy, about 5 minutes.

Meanwhile, add butter to remaining milk in the saucepan; heat over low heat, stirring to melt butter. Pour milk and butter mixture into a large bowl; set aside to cool between 110°F and 115°F. Add remaining 2 Tbsp. of sugar, the salt, yeast mixture, and 3 cups of the flour to the milk mixture. With a wooden spoon, stir to blend completely. Stir in enough additional flour to make dough manageable.

Turn dough out onto a floured surface. Knead dough, adding more flour, if necessary, until smooth and elastic, about 8 to 10 minutes. Place dough in an oiled bowl , turning to oiled side up. Cover with a clean cloth; let dough rise in a warm place, away from drafts, until doubled in size. About one hour.

Grease two 8 ½ x 4 ½ inch loaf pans. Punch dough down. Turn out onto floured surface and cut in half. Shape each half of dough into a 9 inch loaf, or cut each half into three equal parts and roll into a 8 inch rope and braid into a braid, tuck in ends and place into the loaf pans. Cover the loaf pans with a clean cloth and let rise until doubled in size, about one hour.

Heat oven to 350°F.

In a small bowl, beat egg with water and brush loaves with egg mixture and sprinkle with sesame seeds.

Bake loaves 25 to 30 minutes or until golden brown. Remove loaves from pans and let cool completely on a wire rack.

Makes 2 loaves.

Great Garlic Cheese Bread

1 loaf French bread
½ cup butter softened
4 cloves of garlic minced

2 Tbsp. mayonnaise
3 oz. Beer
⅓ jar cheese spread

Slice the French bread in half lengthwise.

In a saucepan on low, mix the garlic with the butter and wisk in the mayonnaise and cheese until well blended. Turn the heat off and add the beer and mix well.

Brown the French bread on the grill until toasty. Soak the toasted side of the bread with the cheese mixture, slice into pieces and enjoy!!!!

This is a recipe from an old friend and his father. They fixed it for Kristina and Dan's wedding dinner. Everyone at the wedding said their wedding was the best they had ever been to, the food was great, and the setting was amazing. It was in the garden of an old Victorian house. When you have the right place, the right food, and the right people you always have a great party.

Challah

2 ½ Tbsp. active dry yeast, 1 pack.
¾ cup milk
¼ cup butter, (½ stick)
2 Tbsp. sugar
2 tsp. salt

4 ½ to 5 cups all-purpose flour
2 eggs
1 egg yolk
1 Tbsp. water
1 Tbsp. sesame seeds

In a small bowl soften the yeast with ½ cup warm water, set aside. Heat the milk, butter, salt, and the sugar until the sugar dissolves; cool to lukewarm. In the bowl of a stand mixer pour in the heated milk and stir in 2 cups of the flour; beat with the paddle attachment, until well mixed. Add the yeast and 2 eggs; beat well. Mix in enough remaining flour to make a soft dough.

Knead with dough hook for 8 minutes, or until the dough no longer sticks to the sides of the bowl, adding more flour if necessary. Turn out onto a floured surface and form a ball. Place dough into a lightly greased bowl, turning once to coat with oil. Cover with plastic wrap and place in a warm spot to rise until double in size, about 1 to 1 ½ hours. Punch down, divide in half, then divide each half into thirds. Cover; let rest for 10 minutes.

Roll each third into a rope 10 inches long. Now take three ropes and braid them, pinching each end together and fit the braid into a greased bread pan. Cover with a clean towel and let rise for about 30 minutes, or until double in size. Brush with egg yolk mixed with 1 Tbsp. water and sprinkle with sesame seeds. Bake in a 375°F oven for 45 to 50 minutes.

Makes 2 loaves.

Sesame Braid

1 ¼ cups milk
3 Tbsp. honey
2 Tbsp. shortening
2 tsp. salt
1 package active dry yeast
¼ cup very warm water
4 cups sifted all-purpose flour
1 egg
1 Tbsp. sesame seeds

Scald milk with honey, shortening, and salt in a small saucepan. Cool until lukewarm. Sprinkle yeast into very warm water in a large mixing bowl. Stir until yeast dissolves and is foamy on top, then stir in cooled milk mixture. Beat in 2 cups of the flour to form a smooth, soft dough. Use the dough hook on the mixer and gradually beat in the remaining 2 cups flour to make a stiff dough.

Knead the dough for about 10 minutes with the dough hook until the dough is smooth and elastic, adding enough extra flour to keep dough from sticking. Place the dough in a greased large bowl, turn to coat both sides, and cover with a clean towel. Let rise in a warm place until doubled in size, about 1 hour.

Punch dough down; knead a few times and divide in half. Divide one half into three equal-size pieces and roll each piece into a rope, 14 inches long. Braid ropes, pinching at ends to hold in place; place braid diagonally on a parchment lined cooky sheet, 15" x 10" x 1". Cut off one-third of the second half of dough and set aside for next step.

Divide remaining into 3 equal-size pieces; roll each into a rope 12 inches long, and braid as before. Place on top of the first braid on the cookie sheet. Repeat dividing into thirds, rolling, and braiding with remaining dough, making a braid about 10 inches long and place on top of the other two braids. Cover and let rise again in a warm place until doubled in size, about an hour. Preheat the oven to 375°F.

When loaf has risen, brush all over with slightly beaten egg and sprinkle with sesame seeds. Bake in oven 45 minutes, or until golden, and the loaf sounds hollow when tapped. If the loaf begins to brown too quickly, place a piece of foil loosely over the top. Remove from the oven and place on a rack to cool completely.

Makes one loaf.

> I have been making this bread for Easter for the last 40 years, and if there is any left the next day it makes great toast.

Hamburger Buns

1 ½ cups warm water
⅔ cup instant powdered milk
⅓ cup melted butter
3 Tbsp. sugar
2 packages active dry yeast
2 large egg yolks

1 large egg
4 ½ - 5 cups all-purpose flour
1 ½ tsp. salt
Olive oil for greasing the bowl
2 Tbsp. milk
2 Tbsp. sesame seeds

Place the warm water, melted butter, dry milk, and sugar in a large bowl of a mixer, and stir to combine with a whisk. Sprinkle the yeast over the mixture, whisk, and let bloom until light and foamy, about 12 minutes.

Add the egg, one egg yolk, 3 cups of flour, and the salt, to the mixer. Use the paddle blade in the mixer and combine until smooth. Switch to the dough hook and add another 1 ½ cups of flour. Knead dough with the dough hook for about 10 minutes, adding the remaining ½ cup flour, if needed.

Turn dough out onto a lightly floured board and knead for 1 minute. Place in a lightly oiled bowl and cover with plastic wrap. Leave in a warm place until doubled in size, about 1 hour. Punch down dough. Turn out onto a lightly floured board and cut in half. Cut each half into six pieces, and form each piece into flattened balls. Arrange balls on two, parchment lined baking sheets, about 3 inches apart. Cover lightly with plastic wrap and place in a warm place until doubled in size, about 45 minutes.

Preheat oven to 400°F. Whisk remaining egg yolk and the 2 Tbsp. of milk together and brush egg wash lightly over buns. Sprinkle the top of the buns with the sesame seeds, if desired. Bake until golden brown, 13 to 15 minutes. Cool on a wire rack. These buns can be frozen for up to 8 months.

Dinner Rolls

⅓ cup honey
1 packet active dry yeast
4 ½ cups all-purpose flour
¼ cup dry buttermilk powder

1 ½ tsp. coarse salt
¼ cup milk
2 large eggs
3 Tbsp. butter, melted

In a small bowl combine ½ cup warm water, ⅓ cup honey, and the yeast. Stir to dissolve the yeast and set aside until mixture becomes bubbly on top, about 5 minutes. In a large bowl, combine 4 cups of the flour, buttermilk powder, and salt; then stir in the yeast mixture. In a small bowl, whisk together the milk, eggs, and 2 Tbsp. melted butter. Stir egg mixture into the flour and combine until dough comes together.

Knead dough on a lightly floured surface or in the bowl of an electric mixer, fitted with a dough hook, for about 8 minutes, adding flour until the dough is smooth. Turn out dough into a lightly oiled bowl and cover with plastic wrap. Let dough rise at room temperature until doubled in size, about 1 hour.

Preheat oven to 375°F. Turn dough out onto a lightly floured board and divide into 4 equal parts, then divide each of those parts into 4 equal parts for a total of 16 pieces. Form the dough into balls. Spray two, 9 inch cake pans with non-stick spray. Place one ball in the middle of each cake pan. Evenly space remaining dough balls around each cake pan. Cover and let rise, at room temperature, for 30 minutes.

In a small bowl melt the 1 tsp. of butter and brush the rolls lightly. Put them into the oven to bake for 20 to 30 minutes, or until golden brown. Let cool for 15 minutes before turning them out onto a wire rack. Serve with butter and honey.

Garlic Cheddar Cheese Biscuits

1 ¼ cups Bisquick baking mix
½ cup sharp cheddar cheese, grated
¼ cup melted butter
¼ tsp. garlic powder
¼ tsp. onion powder
¼ tsp. salt
¼ tsp. dried parsley flakes

Preheat oven to 400°F.

Line a cookie sheet with a parchment paper liner.

Combine the Bisquick, cheese, and the onion powder in a bowl. Add ⅓ cup water and stir until just combined. Drop the dough by tablespoonfuls onto the prepared baking sheet. Bake for about 10 to 12 minutes or until they begin to turn brown.

While the biscuits are baking, make the garlic butter. In a small bowl, mix the melted butter, garlic powder, salt, and parsley flakes together well. With a pastry brush, brush the biscuits with the garlic butter as soon as they come out of the oven.

Makes about 12 biscuits.

The Best Ever Drop Buttermilk Biscuits

2 cups all-purpose flour
1 Tbsp. baking powder
3 tsp. sugar
½ tsp. cream of tartar
½ tsp. salt
¼ tsp. baking soda
½ cup shortening
1 cup buttermilk

In a medium mixing bowl stir together all the dry ingredients. Using a pastry blender, cut the shortening till the mixture resembles coarse crumbs. Make a well in the center of the dry mixture, then add the buttermilk all at once. Using a spoon, stir until just moistened. Drop dough from a tablespoon about 1 inch apart on a greased or parchment lined baking sheet.

Bake in a preheated 450°F oven for 10 to 12 minutes.

Makes about 12 biscuits.

Raised Buttermilk Biscuits

1 package yeast, or 2 ½ tsp.
½ cup lukewarm water
5 cups all-purpose flour
1 tsp. baking soda

2 ½ tsp. salt
1 Tbsp. baking powder
¾ cup shortening
2 cups buttermilk

Dissolve the yeast in the warm water.

Sift the dry ingredients together and cut in the shortening. Add the buttermilk and the yeast and mix well.

Turn the dough out onto a lightly floured board and knead a few times. Roll out to desired thickness and cut with a biscuit cutter or a floured glass and place on a cookie sheet.

Let rest for about 20 minutes, then bake in a 400°F oven for 12 to 15 minutes or until golden brown.

Makes about 15 biscuits.

Buttermilk Biscuits

5 cups all-purpose flour
2 Tbsp. and 1 ½ tsp. Baking powder
1 tsp. baking soda
1 Tbsp. kosher salt

¼ cup cold butter
½ vegetable shortening
2 cups cold buttermilk

Heat oven to 400°F.

In a large bowl whisk together the flour, baking powder, baking soda, and the salt. From this, measure out 3 cups and put into a food processor. Add the butter and shortening, and pulse until the flour is coarsely blended. Transfer the mixture from the food processor back into the bowl with the remaining dry ingredients, and blend well with a whisk.

Make a well in the center and add the buttermilk all at once. With a large spoon stir mixture quickly, just until it is blended and begins to form a sticky dough. Immediately turn dough onto a floured board.

Using floured hands, knead the dough 8 to 10 times until a ball forms. Gently flatten dough with your hands to even thickness. Using a floured rolling pin, lightly roll dough to ¾ inch thickness.

Flour a 2 ½ inch biscuit cutter, or a drinking glass, and cut out biscuits and place them on a parchment-lined baking sheet. Place them on the upper third of the oven and bake them 8-10 minutes, or until golden brown. Serve hot with butter.

Makes 12 to 16 biscuits.

Sour Cream Biscuits

2 cups self-rising flour
1 cup (2 sticks) softened butter
1 tsp. sugar
1 cup sour cream

Preheat oven to 400°F.

Mix the four, sugar, and the butter together; add the sour cream and blend well. Place spoonfuls of the batter into greased muffin tins. I use an ice cream scoop to do this. Bake for 10 to 15 minutes, or until lightly golden brown.

Makes about 15 biscuits.

Cookies

Brownies

¾ cup butter, melted
1 ½ cups sugar
1 ½ tsp. vanilla
3 eggs
1 cup all-purpose flour

½ tsp. baking powder
½ tsp. salt
½ cup chopped nuts
¼ cup cocoa powder

Blend melted butter, sugar, and vanilla in a mixing bowl. Add eggs and beat well with a spoon. In a separate bowl, combine the flour, cocoa, baking powder, and salt. Gradually add in the wet mixture until well blended. Spread into a greased 8-inch square baking pan.

Bake at 350°F for 40 to 45 minutes or until brownie begins to pull away from the edges of the pan. Cool then cut into squares.

Almond Apricot Biscotti

1 cup butter at room temperature
3 cups sugar
4 eggs
6 cups all-purpose flour
2 tsp. baking soda
1 tsp. salt
2 cups toasted almonds- lightly chopped
1 cup dried apricots- chopped into small bits

Take two cookie sheets, place parchment paper on each, then set aside. Set oven at 325°F to preheat.

In a large electric mixer bowl, beat butter and sugar together on medium speed until combined. Beat in eggs, one at a time.

In another large bowl, stir together the baking soda, salt, and flour. At the low setting, beat half of the flour mixture into the butter mixture until combined. Mix in the almonds and the dried apricots, then the remaining flour. Remove the dough to a lightly floured board and knead a few times. Divide the dough into four equal amounts. Shape each piece into a loaf 9 inches by 3 inches. Place two loaves on each cookie sheet.

Bake until the loaves are golden and firm, about 1 hour. Remove from the oven and cool slightly, then move the loaves to a cutting board. Slice crosswise at an angle with a serrated knife, about ½ inch thick. Arrange the slices back onto the baking sheet with the cut side up. Return biscotti slices back to the oven and bake until they are golden and crisp, about 45 minutes. Remove from oven and place on cooling racks to cool completely. Store in air tight container at room temperature for up to 1 week.

Makes about 5 dozen cookies.

Fairy Kisses

4 large egg whites
½ tsp. cream of tartar
¼ tsp. salt

1 cup plus 2 Tbsp. sugar
½ tsp. almond extract
Colored sugar glitter

In a large bowl, combine the egg whites, cream of tartar, and salt. Beat until peaks form, then gradually add the sugar and almond extract, continuing to beat until the mixture is stiff and glossy.

Line two baking sheets with parchment paper. Fit a zip lock plastic bag with a large star pastry tip and fill with the egg white mixture. Press to make star shapes and bake in a pre-heated 200°F oven for 1 ½ hours. Turn the oven off, take the meringues out of the oven and sprinkle with colored sugar glitter and return them to the oven for 3 more hours or overnight, they should be completely dry and cool.

Should make six dozen meringue kisses.

Owl's Eyes

1 cup butter, room temperature
½ cup sugar
½ tsp. vanilla extract
1 ½ tsp. almond extract
1 ¼ cup flour
1 ¼ cup almond flour
½ cup raspberry jam, or apricot jam
2 cups powdered sugar
¼ cup milk

Preheat oven to 350°F. Whisk together the powdered sugar and milk until smooth and the consistency of honey. Put the icing in a zip lock bag and cut a small hole in one of the corners. Set aside until ready to use.

With an electric mixer, beat the sugar, butter, vanilla, and almond extract until light and fluffy. Add the flours, all-purpose and almond, and beat until the dough comes together. With a small ice cream scoop measure out the dough and place the dough on a cookie sheet lined with parchment paper. With the bottom of a very small glass, or the round end of a wooden spoon, press an indentation in the middle of each ball of dough. Put a ¼ tsp. of jam in the middle of each cookie. Bake in the oven for 11 minutes. Remove the cookies from the oven and place on a rack to cool. Once the cookies have cooled, drizzle the icing in a squiggly pattern.

This makes about 4 dozen cookies. Make lots, they don't last long…

I got the idea from a bakery in Solvang, CA. My family just couldn't get enough of them, and at $1.50 each I had to figure out a way to meet their need for Owl's Eyes.

Fruitcake Cookies

1 cup chopped dates
½ cup chopped candied orange peel
1 ½ cups chopped almonds
1 cup golden raisins
5 Tbsp. orange juice
1 Tbsp. honey
1 cup butter, softened to room temperature

½ cup sugar
⅓ cup firmly packed brown sugar
2 Tbsp. orange zest
½ tsp. salt
1 egg, lightly beaten
1 tsp. vanilla
1 tsp. almond extract
2 ⅔ cup flour

In a medium sized bowl, mix the dates, candied orange peel, almonds, raisins, orange juice, and the honey. Cover the bowl with plastic wrap, and let set at room temperature for 8 hours or over night.

Preheat the oven to 350°F.

In the bowl of a stand mixer fitted with a paddle attachment, using medium speed, cream the butter, sugars, orange zest, and salt, until smooth, about 4 minutes. With the mixer at the lowest speed, add the egg, vanilla, almond extract, and mix until well blended. Slowly add the flour and mix until just combined. Add the fruit and nut mixture, and stir to combine. Divide the dough in half. Form each half into an 18 x 2 inch log and place them on some plastic wrap and roll them up and tightly seal. Put them in the fridge for 2 hours, or freeze for up to 6 months.

Line two baking sheets with parchment paper and set aside. Remove the plastic wrap from the cookie log and slice them into ¼ inch thick slices. Put cookies on prepared baking sheets about ½ inches apart.

Bake for 12-14 minutes, or until light golden brown. Remove parchment paper to cooling racks and allow cookies to cool completely. Store in an airtight container for up to 1 week.

If you are freezing the cookie dough remove the logs from the freezer and let thaw for 10 minutes before slicing.

This make about 120 cookies.

Oatmeal Chocolate Chip Cookies

1 cup all-purpose flour
¼ tsp. baking powder
¼ tsp. baking soda
¼ tsp. ground cinnamon
½ salt
1 stick butter (½ cup)
at room temperature

⅔ cup packed brown sugar
⅓ cup granulated sugar
1 egg
1 tsp. vanilla
1 ½ cups rolled oats
½ raisins
1 cup mini chocolate chips

Preheat oven to 350°F.

Sift flour, baking powder, baking soda, salt, and oats into a bowl. Beat butter and sugars until fluffy. Mix in egg and vanilla, then flour mixture. Add raisins and chocolate chips.

Using a 1 ¼ inch ice cream scoop, drop dough onto a baking sheet, about 2 inches apart. Bake until edges are golden, about 14 min. Remove to a wire cooling rack.

Makes about 5 dozen cookies.

Chocolate Chip Shortbread Cookies

1 cup butter, softened
½ cup powdered sugar
½ cup sugar
1 egg
1 tsp. almond extract

2 ¼ cups all-purpose flour
½ tsp. baking soda
½ tsp. cream of tartar
Extra sugar
2 cups mini chocolate chips

Heat oven to 375°F. Mix together the butter, powered sugar, and granulated sugar in a mixing bowl and beat until creamy, scraping the sides of the bowl often. Add the egg and almond extract, continue beating until well mixed. Add the flour, the baking soda, and the cream of tartar, and beat until the dough forms a ball. Add the chocolate chips and mix in well.

Using a small ice cream scoop, form dough into 1 inch balls. Dip into extra sugar and place on a ungreased cookie sheet. With the bottom of a small glass, dipped in sugar, flatten the dough ball. Bake for 7 to 9 minutes or until lightly browned around the edges. Let cool for 1 minute and remove to cooling rack.

Makes 4 dozen cookies.

Jumbo Oatmeal Cookies

1 ½ cups all-purpose flour
1 cup butter (two sticks) softened
1 ¼ cups sugar
¼ cup brown sugar (packed)
2 tsp. vanilla

1 ½ tsp. baking soda
1 tsp. salt
2 large eggs
3 ½ cups old-fashion oats, uncooked

Into a large bowl, mix the butter and sugars until creamy. Add the flour, vanilla, baking soda, and salt and mix well. Add the oats and mix until just blended. With a 2" ice cream scoop, scoop the dough onto a baking sheet about 2" apart.

Bake in a 375°F. oven until golden brown, 15 to 17 minutes.

Carefully remove cookies to a cooling rack. Store cookies in a tightly covered container.

Makes about 1 ½ dozen.

If you want, you can add ¾ cup raisins, dried cranberry, or dried cherrys.

Chocolate Oatmeal Cookies

2 cups butter (at room temperature)
4 cups all-purpose flour
2 tsp. baking soda
2 cups sugar
5 cups oatmeal
24 oz chocolate chips
2 cups brown sugar

1 tsp. salt
8 oz. chocolate bar (grated)
4 eggs
2 tsp. baking powder
2 tsp. vanilla
2 cups chopped nuts (optional)

Measure oatmeal and blend in a blender to a fine powder. Cream the butter and both the sugars. In a large mixing bowl add the eggs and the vanilla, and mix together with the flour, oatmeal, salt, baking soda, and baking powder. Add the chocolate chips, chocolate bar, and the nuts; then mix well. Scoop the cookie dough with an ice cream scoop onto a cookie sheet about two inches apart.

Bake 10 minutes at 375°F.

Makes about 112 cookies.

Chocolate Cookies

1 ¼ cups butter, softened
2 cups sugar
2 eggs
2 tsp. vanilla
2 cups unsifted all-purpose flour

¾ cocoa powder
1 tsp. baking soda
½ tsp. salt
1 cup finely chopped nuts (optional)

Cream the butter and sugar in a large mixer bowl. Add the eggs and the vanilla until well blended. Combine the flour, cocoa, baking soda, and salt. Add to the creamed mixture and combine well. Stir in the nuts if desired. Drop by tablespoonfuls onto a cookie sheet. Bake in a preheated 350°F oven for 8 to 9 minutes. Do not over bake. Cool on the cookie sheet for 1 minute then remove to a wire rack to cool completely.

Makes about 4 dozen.

Old Fashioned Sugar Cookies

3 cups all-purpose flour
1 tsp. baking soda
¼ tsp. salt
1 ¾ cups sugar
¼ cup packed light brown sugar
1 Tbsp. lemon zest

1 Tbsp. fresh lemon juice
1 tsp. vanilla
1 cup butter softened
2 large eggs
Sugar for sprinkling

Preheat oven to 350°F. Mix flour, baking soda, and salt in a bowl with a wisk. Put the sugars and lemon zest in the bowl of an electric mixer with a paddle attachment. Mix on medium speed for about 1 minute. Add the butter and mix until fluffy. Mix in eggs, one at a time, then the lemon juice and vanilla. Gradually add the flour mixture, and mix until just combined. With an ice cream scoop place the cookies on the cookie sheet and flatten cookies with the bottom of a glass dipped into sugar. Sprinkle with additional sugar and brush lightly with a pastry brush dipped into water. Bake cookies for about 15 minutes or until lightly golden brown. Transfer cookies to cooling racks to cool completely.

Makes about 20 3-inch cookies.

> This recipe is the closest I have found to the taste of the sugar cookies my grandpa LeClair used to buy me when I was a little girl. It's funny how a taste can stay with you your whole life and you know it's just right the minute you taste it. The flood of memories come rushing back no matter how old you are.

Rice Krispie Cookies

1 cup sugar
1 cup brown sugar
1 cup vegetable shortening
2 eggs
1 ¾ cup sifted flour
1 tsp. baking powder
1 tsp. baking soda
1 tsp. salt
1 tsp. vanilla
1 cup oatmeal
2 cups Rice Krispies

Using an electric mixer, cream shortening and sugars. Add unbeaten eggs, one at a time. Sift dry ingredients and add to sugar mixture. Add vanilla, oats, and Rice Krispies, and mix all together.

Drop by tablespoonful on an ungreased cookie sheet.

Bake in 350°F oven for 10-12 minutes.

Makes about 8 dozen.

Granny's Molasses Cookies

¾ cup Crisco shortening
1 cup brown sugar
1 egg
4 Tbsp. molasses
¼ tsp. salt

2 ¼ cups flour
2 tsp. baking soda
½ tsp. ground gloves
1 tsp. cinnamon
1 tsp. ground ginger

Cream shortening with the brown sugar. Add the eggs and molasses and blend well. Add all the rest and mix well. Chill one hour.

Shape into balls and dip top into sugar. Place sugar side up on a ungreased baking sheet and flatten with the bottom of a glass.

Bake in a 375°F oven for 12-15 min.

This was Waive Nance Long LeClair's recipe, she was also known as Own Mama. Everyone in the family loved these cookies. I made them one year and entered them into the Ventura County Fair and won a blue ribbon for them. I gave the ribbon to Own Mama which made her very happy, she said this was the first Blue Ribbon she had ever won.

Oatmeal Cookies
with dried cranberries

2 cups oats
1 ½ cups all-purpose flour
1 tsp. ground cinnamon
½ tsp. salt
½ tsp. baking powder
½ tsp. baking soda

1 cup butter (2 sticks) room temperature
1 cup firmly packed brown sugar
½ cup granulated sugar
2 large eggs
1 tsp. vanilla
2 cups dried cranberries

Preheat oven to 350°F. In a medium bowl, combine the flour, salt, cinnamon, baking soda, and baking powder then set aside.

Using an electric mixer, beat the butter and the sugars until light and fluffy.

Add the eggs and vanilla, and beat until combined.

On low speed, add the flour mixture and the oats; mix until combined.

Stir in the dried cranberries.

Using a 2 ounce ice cream scoop, drop the dough onto a cookie sheet about 3 inches apart. Bake cookies about 15 minutes or until the edges are just turning brown. Place on a wire rack until completely cooled.

Makes about 4 dozen.

Raspberry Slices

½ cup butter at room temperature
¼ cup sugar
1 tsp. vanilla

1 ¼ cups all-purpose flour
¼ cup raspberry jam
2 ounces white chocolate chips

Preheat oven to 350°F.

In a large bowl of a mixer beat the butter, sugar, and vanilla until smooth. Stir in the flour and beat until the dough comes together. Divide the dough into thirds.

On a floured surface roll each portion into a 9" long rope, about 1-inch thick. Place the three ropes 3" apart on a cookie sheet lined with parchment paper. Press your finger into dough to make a ½ inch wide trough all along the rope. Spoon raspberry jam into each of the rope troughs.

Bake ropes in a 350°F oven until edges are lightly browned; 12 to 15 min. Let cool on baking sheet.

Seal white chocolate chips in a plastic zip-lock sandwich bag, close top and place bag into a cup of hot water until chips are melted. Dry bag, then, with scissors, cut off the corner.

Squeeze the bag to drizzle the white chocolate across the cooled ropes. Chill the ropes until the chocolate is firm to the touch then cut them into 12 slices, on the diagonal.

Butter Pecan Crisps

2 ½ cups brown sugar
1 cup butter, softened
1 tsp. vanilla
2 eggs
3 cups all-purpose flour

½ tsp. baking soda
½ tsp. salt
1 cup pecans, chopped and toasted
3 Tbsp. granulated sugar

Beat brown sugar and butter until well blended then add vanilla and eggs. Add flour, baking soda, salt, and pecans. Mix well.

Shape into 1" balls and place 2" apart on ungreased sheet. Flatten balls with the bottom of a glass dipped into sugar.

Bake at 375°F for 8-10 min. or until edges are golden. Cool on baking sheet for 1 minute then remove to a wire rack to cool completely.

Makes about 4 dozen cookies.

Chewy Chocolate Cookies

1 ¼ cups butter, softened
2 cups sugar
2 eggs
2 tsp. vanilla

2 cups unsifted all-purpose flour
¾ cup cocoa powder
1 tsp. baking soda
½ tsp. salt

Cream the butter and sugar in a large mixer bowl. Add the eggs and vanilla and blend well.

Combine the flour, cocoa, baking soda, and the salt and mix in with the creamed butter mixture. Drop by tablespoonfuls onto ungreased baking sheet.

Bake at 350°F for 9-10 min. Do not over bake.

Cool on baking sheet for about 2 minutes, then remove to a wire rack to cool completely.

Makes about 4 dozen Cookies.

Peanut Butter Cookies

¾ cup peanut butter
½ cup vegetable shortening
1 ¼ cup brown sugar-packed
3 Tbsp. milk
1 Tbsp. vanilla

1 egg
1 ¾ cup all-purpose flour
¾ tsp. salt
¾ tsp. baking soda

Heat oven to 375°F.

Combine peanut butter, vegetable shortening, brown sugar, milk, and vanilla in a large bowl, and beat until well blended. Add egg and mix well.

Combine flour, salt, and baking soda and add to creamed mixture. Mix well.

Drop by tablespoonful and roll into a ball and place on an ungreased baking sheet. With a fork dipped into sugar, press into cookie to flatten and make a criss-cross pattern.

Bake for 10-12 minutes or until lightly browned.

Makes about 3 dozen cookies.

Sugar Cookies

1 cup butter
1 ½ cups powered sugar
1 egg
1 tsp. vanilla
2 ½ sifted flour

1 tsp. baking soda
1 tsp. cream of tartar
¼ salt

Preheat oven to 350°F.

Mix sugar and butter until fluffy. Add unbeaten egg and vanilla. Sift dry ingredients together and mix with butter mixture.

Flour a board and roll dough out. Cut into shapes and put onto an ungreased baking sheet.

Bake for 10-12 minutes, or until lightly browned on edges.

Remove from oven and put on cooling racks until cool.

Desserts

Cream Cheese Pound Cake

1 ⅓ cups butter, room temperature
8 oz. cream cheese, room temperature
3 cups sugar
6 large eggs

1 tsp. vanilla
3 cups all-purpose flour
2 tsp. salt
Nonstick cooking spray

Preheat oven to 350°F.

With an electric mixer beat butter and cream cheese until smooth. Add sugar and beat until light and fluffy; about 8 minutes. Add eggs one at a time, beating well after each egg. Add vanilla and mix well. With mixer on low, add flour and salt in three additions, beating until just combined.

Generously coat two 8 ½" x 4 ½" x 2 ½" loaf pans with cooking spray, or use one bundt pan. Pour in batter. Tap pans on work surface to eliminate any large bubbles. Bake until golden, or when a toothpick inserted in the center comes out clean; 60 to 75 minutes. Cool 10 minutes in the pan.

Turn out the cakes and cool completely with top sides up, on a wire rack.

Almond Tart Crust

1 cup butter (2 sticks) room temperature
¾ cup confectioner's sugar
2 cups all-purpose flour
½ tsp. salt
¼ cup almond paste

With a standing mixer on medium speed, beat the butter, sugar and the almond paste until pale yellow and fluffy, about 3 minutes. Reduce speed to medium-low. Add the flour and salt, and beat until just combined and crumbly. Shape dough into a 9-inch disk, and wrap in plastic. Refrigerate at least 30 minutes. When ready to bake press dough into a tart pan with a removable bottom, making it about ¼ inch thick. Refrigerate for about 10 minutes.

Preheat oven to 350°F. Line tart shell with parchment paper, and fill with dried beans or pie weights. Bake until edges are golden brown, about 20 minutes. Remove from oven and remove parchment paper and pie weights. Bake again until bottom is crisp and lightly golden, about another 10 to 15 minutes. Let cool on a wire rack for 10 minutes.

Pastry Cream

1 cup milk
¼ cup granulated sugar
3 Tbsp. all-purpose flour
¼ tsp. salt

4 egg yolks
2 tsp. vanilla extract
2 Tbsp. butter

To make the pastry cream, heat the milk in a heavy saucepan until hot, but not boiling. Combine the sugar, flour, and salt in a mixing bowl, and slowly add the hot milk. Pour this mixture back into the saucepan and bring to a boil over low heat, stirring constantly. Cook the mixture until smooth and very thick.

Remove from heat and beat in the egg yolks, one at a time. Return the mixture to the heat and boil for about one minute, stirring quickly. Remove from the heat and continue to beat until the mixture cools slightly. Stir in the vanilla and butter, blending thoroughly. Cover the pastry cream with plastic wrap directly touching the cream and let cool completely in the regfrigerator.

This pastry cream is great for the base of a fruit tart.

Cream Cheese Frosting

1 lb. cream cheese, room temperature
6 Tbsp. butter, room temperature
1 ¼ cups powdered sugar
1 ½ tsp. vanilla extract

In a large bowl of an electric mixer fitted with the paddle attachment, combine the cream cheese with the butter at medium-high speed. Reduce the speed to very low and add the powdered sugar and beat until smooth. Add the vanilla and blend well.

Chocolate Sour Cream Frosting

¼ cup butter
¼ cup heavy cream
10 oz. bittersweet chocolate, chopped

¾ cup sour cream
1 cup powdered sugar

In a medium-sized saucepan over low heat, combine the butter and the cream. Heat, stirring frequently, until the butter melts. Add the chocolate and whisk until the chocolate is melted and smooth. Remove from the heat and let cool to barely lukewarm, about 10 minutes. Whisk in the sour cream until completely combined, then whisk in the powdered sugar. Let stand until thick enough to spread. If the frosting becomes to thick rewarm briefly over low heat and whisk again until smooth.

Makes about 2 ½ cups.

Lemon Poppy Seed Pound Cake

1 package lemon cake mix
1 package lemon instant pudding mix
4 eggs
⅓ cup vegetable oil
½ cup lemon flavor frosting
4 Tbsp. poppy seeds
1 cup water
1 container lemon frosting
¼ cup fresh lemon juice

Preheat oven to 350°F.

Grease and flour 10-inch bundt pan. Combine the cake mix, pudding mix, eggs, water, and oil in a large mixing bowl. Beat at medium speed with electric mixer for 2 min. Add poppy seeds and mix well.

Pour into pan and bake for 50 to 60 minutes or until a toothpick inserted in center comes out clean. Cool in pan for 25 min. Invert onto serving plate. Cool completely.

For glaze, heat frosting in a small saucepan over medium heat, stirring constantly until thin. Mix in ¼ cup lemon juice, then drizzle over cake.

Cheesecake

Crust-
2 ½ cups graham cracker crumbs
¾ cups melted butter
3 Tbsp. sugar

Filling-
16 oz. cream cheese, softened
1 cup sugar
2 Tbsp. lemon juice
½ tsp. vanilla extract
Dash of salt
4 eggs

Topping-
1 ½ cups sour cream
3 Tbsp. sugar
¾ tsp. vanilla

Crust
Combine and press into a 9 inch springform pan, building up the sides. Bake in a 325°F oven for 10 min.

Filling
Beat softened cream cheese until fluffy. Gradually blend in sugar, lemon juice, vanilla, and salt. Add eggs, one at a time; beat after each. Pour filling into crust. Bake at 325°F for 25-30 min, or until set.

Topping
Combine all ingredients and spoon over top of hot cheesecake. Bake for 10 more minutes. Let chill several hours.

Serves eight.

Great Chocolate Cake

2 cups sugar
¾ cups cocoa
1 ¾ cup all-purpose flour
1 ½ tsp. baking soda
1 ½ tsp. salt

2 eggs
1 cup milk
½ cup vegetable oil
2 tsp. vanilla
1 cup boiling water

Pre-heat oven to 350°F.

Grease two 9" round cake pans. Combine all the dry ingredients in a large bowl. Add the eggs, milk, oil, and vanilla and beat on medium for 2 minutes. Stir in boiling water and mix well.

Pour into the cake pans and bake for 30-35 minutes or until a toothpick stuck in the center comes out clean. Remove from oven and cool in pans for 10 minutes. Remove from pans and cool on cooling racks until completely cool.

Frost with Great Chocolate Frosting.*

*For Great Chocolate Frosting see following page.

Great Chocolate Frosting

1 stick butter (½ cup)
3 cups powdered sugar
⅔ cup cocoa
⅓ cup milk
1 tsp. vanilla

Melt the butter and stir in cocoa. Alternately add powdered sugar and milk. Beat on medium speed to spreading consistency. Add more milk if necessary. Stir in vanilla.

Flourless Chocolate Cake

8 large eggs, cold
1 pound bittersweet, or semisweet chocolate - chopped
½ pound butter, cut into ½ inch chunks

¼ cup strong coffee or orange juice
¼ cup sugar
Confectioners' sugar or cocoa powder for decoration

Preheat oven to 325°F.

Line the bottom of an 8-inch springform pan with parchment paper and grease pan sides. Cover pan underneath and along sides with sheets of heavy-duty aluminum foil and set wrapped pan in a large roasting pan. Bring a kettle of water to boil.

Beat eggs in a bowl of electric mixer fitted with a wire whip attachment for about 5 minutes. Add sugar half way through mixing.

Meanwhile, melt chocolate and butter in a bowl that's been set on top of a pan of simmering water, you can now add the coffee or orange juice. Heat chocolate mixture to 115°F. Using a large rubber spatula, fold ⅓ of the egg foam into the chocolate mixture until only a few streaks of egg are visible; fold in half of the remaining egg mixture, then the other half. Mix until combined completely.

Pour batter into the prepared springform pan. Place the roasting pan into the oven and pour the boiling water into the roasting pan. Bake until the cake has risen slightly, and an instant-read thermometer inserted half way through the center reads 140°F.; 22 to 25 minutes. Remove springform pan from the water bath and set on wire rack to cool. Cover and refrigerate overnight.

About 30 minutes before serving, remove springform pan sides, invert cake on a sheet of waxed paper, peel off parchment paper liner, and turn cake right-side up on a serving platter. Sieve a light sprinkling of confectioners sugar or unsweetened cocoa powder over cake to decorate.

No Flour Lemon Pie

4 large eggs, separated, at room temperature
½ tsp. cream of tartar
¾ tsp. salt
1 ½ cups sugar

1 Tbsp. grated lemon zest
3 Tbsp. lemon juice
2 cups heavy whipping cream, chilled

Adjust oven rack to middle position and heat oven to 300°F. Grease a 9 inch deep-dish pie plate.

In a large bowl, whip the egg whites, cream of tartar, and ½ tsp. salt with the whisk attachment on medium-low speed until foamy, about 1 minute. Increase to medium-high speed and whip whites to soft, billowy mounds, 1-3 minutes. Gradually whip in 1 cup sugar, about 1 minute. Continue to whip until whites are glossy and very stiff, 3-6 minutes.

Spread meringue into prepared pie dish and smooth into even layer. Run your thumb around the edge of the pie plate to create a small gap between the meringue and the rim of the plate. Bake the meringue until golden and set, about 1 hour. Turn off the oven and let meringue dry completely for 3 hours longer. Let meringue cool completely on wire rack, about 30 minutes.

Meanwhile, whisk egg yolks, lemon zest, lemon juice, remaining ¼ tsp. salt, and remaining ½ cup sugar together in a medium saucepan until smooth. Cook over medium-low heat stirring constantly, until mixture thickens slightly (about 170°F. on instant read thermometer), about 5 minutes. Strain lemon curd through a fine-mesh strainer into a large bowl cover with plastic wrap, pressing wrap directly onto surface. Refrigerate lemon curd until cooled completely, about 1 hour.

Whip cream in a large bowl of mixer on medium-high speed until frothy. Increase speed to high and continue to whip until cream forms soft peaks. Fold half of whipped cream into cooled lemon curd until no white streaks remain. Spread lemon mixture into cooled meringue shell and smooth into even layer. Spread remaining whipped cream attractively over top and chill until filling and topping have set, about 1 hour, before serving.

Pie Crust Dough

2 cups all-purpose flour
1 tsp. salt
⅔ cup shortening
5 to 7 Tbsp. ice cold water

Mix together flour and salt. Cut in shortening with a pastry blender or a fork until pieces are the size of peas. Sprinkle in the cold water, till the dough sticks together and form a ball. Be careful not to add too much water. Cut ball of dough into two pieces. On a lightly floured board roll one half of the dough to an ⅛ of an inch thick. If edges split, pinch together. Always roll going from center to the edge of the dough. Use light strokes. To transfer the pastry, roll it over the rolling pin; unroll pastry over the pie plate, fitting loosely onto the bottom and sides.

This recipe will make enough pastry to make two single pie shells, or one 9' or 10' double-crust pie.

Apple Pie

6 or 7 tart apples, peeled
¾ to 1 cup sugar
2 Tbsp. all-purpose flour
1 tsp. cinnamon

Dash of nutmeg
¼ tsp. salt
2 Tbsp. of butter
Pastry for 2-crust 9-inch pie*

Pare apples and slice very thin. Combine sugar, flour, spices, and salt; mix with apples. Line a 9 inch pie plate with the pie dough, fill with the apple mixture, and crumble butter into small peices over top. Place the top crust, and crimp the edges tight so the filling won't leak out. Sprinkle with sugar for sparkle. Place the pie plate on a rimmed cookie sheet.

Bake in a hot (400°F) oven for about 50 minutes or until done.

*For pie crust, see page 113.

Pumpkin Pie

1 ½ cups sugar
1 tsp. salt
2 tsp. ground cinnamon
1 tsp. ground ginger
⅛ tsp. ground cloves

4 large eggs
1 can (29 oz.) pumpkin
2 cans evaporated milk
2 unbaked 9-inch pie shells*

Mix sugar, salt, cinnamon, ginger, and cloves in a large bowl. Beat the eggs in a small bowl. In the larger bowl mix the dry ingredients, the beaten eggs, the pumpkin, and the milk and whisk until all the ingredients are thoroughly mixed.

Pour the pumpkin mixture into the pie shells and bake in a preheated oven at 425°F for 15 minutes. Reduce the temperature to 350°F; bake 40-50 minutes more or until a knife inserted in the center of the pie comes out clean.

Cool on a wire rack for 2 hours. Serve immediately or refrigerate.

*For pie crust, see page 113.

Peach Crisp

12 peaches, peeled and sliced
1 tsp. lemon zest
¼ cup maple syrup
2 cups flour
1 cup sugar
1 cup brown sugar
1 tsp. ground cinnamon
¼ tsp. ground nutmeg
½ tsp. salt
2 sticks of cold butter, cubed

Mix the peaches with the lemon zest and the maple syrup and put into a large baking dish.

For the topping mix the flour, sugars, cinnamon, nutmeg, and salt into a large bowl and cut in the butter with a pastry cutter until it looks like cornmeal. Sprinkle on top of the peaches and cover with foil and bake in a 350°F oven for 15 minutes. Remove the foil and bake for another 30 to 40 minutes or until lightly brown and bubbly. Serve warm or room temperature with a maple cream sauce.*

*For maple cream sauce, see following page.

Maple Cream Sauce

3 cups heavy whipping cream
¾ cup maple syrup
⅓ cup corn syrup
½ tsp. salt

In a saucepan combine the 4 ingredients and over medium heat bring to a boil. Boiling for 20 minutes or until the mixture has reduced by about ⅓ and is thick and creamy. Pour into a container and chill for one hour or over night. Pour over the individual servings of peach crisp. This maple cream sauce is great poured over just about anything!!!

Incredible Fruit Cobbler

1 tsp. baking powder
1 cup vanilla sugar*
1 cup all-purpose flour
4 cups berries or peeled & chopped peaches
¼ cup orange juice

2 tsp. cornstarch
¼ cup sugar
1 tsp. cinnamon
1 cup melted butter
1 egg

Mix all the dry ingrediens together and set aside. Blend the orange juice with the cornstarch and pour over the fruit. Pour the fruit into a 9" x 13" baking dish and sprinkle on the ¼ cup sugar. Combine the melted butter with the egg and pour in the flour mixture, mix well. Drop the cobbler by tablespoonfuls over the fruit mixture. Sprinkle the cinnamon over the top and bake in a 375°F oven for 40 minutes, or until golden in color. Serve warm with vanilla ice cream if desired.

Makes 12 servings.

*I make vanilla sugar by drying used vanilla beans that I've used to make ice cream, and putting them into a pint jar with sugar. Seal the jar and leave on the shelf until ready to use. The longer it's stored, the more flavor is imparted into the sugar.

Pumpkin Custard Squares

1 package yellow cake mix
½ cup butter, softened
3 eggs
1 large can (29 oz.) pumpkin
⅔ cup milk
½ tsp. of each: Ground allspice, ground cloves, ground ginger, and salt.
1 tsp. ground cinnamon
¼ tsp. ground nutmeg
½ cup brown sugar, firmly packed
¼ cup butter, softened
1 cup chopped nuts (pecans or walnuts if desired)

Empty cake mix into a bowl; cut in the ½ cup butter until mixture forms moist, even crumbs; reserve 1 cup of the crumb mixture for the topping. Add to the remaining crumb mixture 1 of the eggs; stir until blended. Spoon this into the bottom of a greased 9 by 13 inch baking pan and press lightly to form an even layer. Bake in a 350°F oven for 10 minutes, or until puffy; set aside.

Meanwhile, beat remaining 2 eggs until foamy. Gradually beat in the pumpkin and milk. Stir in the allspice, cloves, ginger, salt, ½ tsp. of cinnamon, nutmeg, and ¼ cup of the brown sugar; pour on top of the baked cake layer. Combine the reserved 1 cup of the crumb mixture with the remaining ½ tsp. cinnamon and ¼ cup brown sugar; add the ¼ cup butter and stir until blended. Stir in the nuts, if desired. Drop by spoonfuls to form an even layer of crumbs on top of the pumpkin batter.

Bake in a 350°F oven until custard is slightly "set" in the center, about 30 minutes; let cool completely. Shortly before serving, cut into 3-inch squares and top with whipped cream.

Makes 12 to 15 servings.

Pumpkin Cheesecake

Crust
1 ½ cups graham cracker crumbs
¼ cup granulated sugar
⅓ cup melted butter
¼ tsp. cinnamon

Filling
24oz. Cream cheese, softened
1 cup granulated sugar
¼ cup light brown sugar, packed
1 ¾ cups solid pack pumpkin (16 oz. can)
2 eggs
⅔ cup evaporated milk, undiluted
2 Tbsp. cornstarch
1 ¼ tsp. ground cinnamon

Crust:
Combine the graham cracker crumbs, sugar, cinnamon, and butter in a medium bowl. Press into the bottom and up the sides of a 9 inch springform pan. Bake in a preheated 350°F oven for 9-10 minutes. Remove from oven and let cool while you mix the filling.

Filling:
Beat the cream cheese, granulated sugar, and brown sugar in a large mixing bowl until fluffy. Beat in the pumpkin, eggs, and evaporated milk. Add the cornstarch, cinnamon, and nutmeg; beat well. Pour into crust. Bake in 350°F oven for about 55 to 60 minutes or until the edge is set.

For the topping, mix together 2 cups sour cream, ¼ cup granulated sugar, and 1 tsp. vanilla until smooth. Spread over warm cheesecake and return to 350°F oven for another 5 minutes. Cool on wire rack. Chill for several hours, then remove the sides of the pan to serve.

Makes 12 servings.

Crock Pot Apple Pie Cake

1 box spice cake mix
2 sticks of butter
2 cans apple pie filling (20 oz cans) or 2 quarts of my canned apple pie filling*

In the crock pot empty the apple pie filling, spread out evenly. On top of that add the dry cake mix, spread that out evenly too. On top of that add the 2 sticks of butter. Put the lid on and turn on the crock pot to high and cook for 3 hours. It is as easy as that! It is delicious. Also great with a big old scoop of vanilla ice cream. Serve this warm.

*For apple pie filling, see page 145.

Chocolate Banana Nut Bread

6 Tbsp. butter (at room temperature)
1 cup sugar
2 or 3 very ripe bananas, mashed
3 large eggs, slightly beaten
½ cup buttermilk
2 cups all-purpose flour
⅓ cup cocoa powder
1 tsp. baking soda
1 tsp. baking powder
½ tsp. salt
1 cup chocolate chips

Preheat oven to 350°F. Grease and lightly flour a 9 x 5 inch loaf pan.

In a heavy-duty mixer fitted with a paddle attachment, beat together the butter and sugar on medium speed until creamy, about 1 minute. Add the bananas and eggs and beat until smooth. Add the buttermilk and mix just until combined.

In a bowl, stir the flour, cocoa powder, baking soda, baking powder, and salt. Add the dry ingredients to the banana mixture and beat until just combined, and fold in the chocolate chips. The batter will be a little lumpy.

Pour the batter in the loaf pan; it should be no more than ⅔rd full. Bake until the loaf is a dark golden brown; about 55-60 minutes. A cake tester inserted into the center should come out clean. Let rest in the pan for about 5 minutes, then turn out onto a wire rack to cool completely.

Cut into slices about ½ inch thick.

Banana Bread

½ cup butter, softened
1 cup sugar
½ tsp. salt
2 eggs
1 tsp. vanilla

1 ½ cups all-purpose flour
1 tsp. baking soda
1 tsp. baking powder
3 ripe bananas, mashed

Preheat the oven to 350°F. Grease one 9 x 5 inch loaf pan. In a mixing bowl, combine the butter and sugar; mix well. Add the salt, eggs, vanilla, flour, baking soda, baking powder, and the bananas, then mix well. Pour the mixture into the prepared baking pan and bake for 50 minutes. It is done when a tooth pick stuck in the center comes out dry.

Makes one loaf and only dirties one bowl for mixing. So, Easy clean up!

Dutch Baby Pancake

4 eggs
1 cup milk
1 cup flour
½ cup butter

Heat oven to 425°F.

Put butter in a 9" cast iron frying pan and put in the oven until the butter is melted and bubbling. Beat the four eggs in a blender, adding the milk and the flour a third at a time, ending with the milk. Pour the batter into the frying pan and bake for 25 minutes. The pancake will rise up the sides of the pan and will be a pretty golden color. Remove the pancake from the oven and cut into wedges and serve with warmed maple syrup.

You can also serve with fresh berries and bacon and sausage.

Danish Pastry (Aage Nagel)

First dough:
2 cups flour
1 cup butter

Second dough:
1 cup butter
2 cups sifted flour
6 Eggs

2 cups water
2 tsp. almond extract

Topping:
4 cups powdered sugar
1 tsp. almond extract
¼ cup milk
2 cups toasted slivered almonds
1 can cherry pie filling

First dough:
In a food processor cut the butter and flour together like a pie crust. Add four Tbsp. of water to dough and mix. Let dough rest for 10 minutes. Cut into four pieces and place two of each on two cookie sheets. Roll dough into strips and flatten with the palms of your hand to 4" wide and 10" long.

Second dough:
Bring butter and water to a boil in a large saucepan. Add 2 tsp. almond extract and remove from the heat. Add 2 cups of flour and stir to form a ball. Add the six eggs, one at a time, beating each egg in until the dough is smooth. At this time place about ⅔ cup of the cherry pie filling on top of the first dough, right in the middle and not quite to the ends. Now divide the second dough into four equal parts and spread on top of cherry pie filling covering it completely. Bake in a 350°F oven for about 60 minutes, or until lightly browned.

Topping:
Mix powered sugar, almond extract, and milk together and drizzle over Danish and sprinkle with toasted almonds.

Makes 4 Danishes.

This recipe was given to me by a missionary in our church ward. I only make the danish on Christmas Eve for our Christmas breakfast. We also give some to special friends for their Christmas morning. I usually make about twelve each year and that is all until next Christmas.

Panna Cotta with Raspberry Sauce

1 ⅔ cups whipping cream
1 envelope unflavored gelatin
2 cups fresh raspberries, rinsed and stemmed
1 ¾ cup sugar
1 cup water
1 cup buttermilk

In a medium sized saucepan, stir together ⅔ cup whipping cream and the gelatin; let stand 5 minutes. Stir over medium heat until the gelatin dissolves. Stir in the remaining whipping cream, buttermilk, and ¾ cup sugar. Stir until an instant-read thermometer registers 160°F. Pour into 6 custard cups, cover and chill for 4 to 24 hours.

For the berry sauce combine the raspberries, 1 cup sugar, and water in a small saucepan. Bring to a boil. Reduce the heat and simmer, uncovered, for 10 minutes or until slightly thickened. Strain mixture through a fine sieve or a food mill, to remove seeds. Cover and chill sauce for up to 24 hours before serving.

To serve, spoon some sauce onto individual serving dishes. To unmold the panna cotta, hold each dish under warm water to slightly soften. Run a knife around the edge. Unmold over the sauce on the dish. Spoon additional sauce over the panna cotta.

Serves 6.

This is a favorite dessert of my daughter Kristina. We had it at an Italian restaurant and she loved it so much, I found a recipe for it so I can make it for her anytime.

Own Mama's Banana Pudding

1 ½ cups sugar
½ cup all-purpose flour
4 cups milk
6 egg yolks

2 tsp. vanilla
4 Tbsp. butter (½ stick)
5 medium bananas, sliced
1 box of vanilla wafers

In a medium sized saucepan mix the sugar and flour together, then slowly mix in the milk. Over low heat cook and stir the mixture until it becomes thick; do not leave the pan until it becomes thick. Slightly beat the egg yolks and temper with a small amount of the hot custard making sure you are stirring well. Add the egg mixture to the custard pan and cook 3 more minutes. Remove the pan from the heat and add the vanilla and butter. Let cool.

In a large casserole dish, alternate pudding, bananas, and the wafers, beginning with the pudding and ending with the pudding. Place in refrigerator until cool then top with whipped cream.

Serves 8 to 10.

Own Mama's Custard

4 eggs
½ cup sugar
2 cups milk
½ cup cream
1 tsp. vanilla
½ tsp. salt
1 tsp. grated nutmeg

In a small saucepan heat milk and cream to 100°F. Meanwhile, in a medium sized bowl beat eggs, sugar, salt, and vanilla together. When the milk is warm, slowly whisk into egg mixture, until well combined. Heat some water until very hot and set aside. Get a large cookie sheet and place a 9" x 13" baking dish on it.

Place six custard cups in the baking dish. Ladle the hot custard mixture into the cups. Now place the cookie sheet into a 325°F oven and pour the hot water into the baking dish, being careful not to get any water into the cups. Sprinkle some grated nutmeg over the custard. Very carefully slide the oven rack back into the oven and bake for 45 minutes, or until a knife inserted comes out clean. Let cool, then store covered in the fridge.

Chocolate Gravy

1 cup sugar
3 Tbsp. flour
3 Tbsp. cocoa powder
1 cup milk

½ cup heavy cream
½ cup water
¼ tsp. salt
1 tsp. vanilla

In a saucepan combine the dry ingredients; flour, sugar, cocoa powder, and salt. Whisk until well blended. Next add the milk, cream, and the water, and over medium heat cook until it begins to thicken. Remove from the heat and stir in the vanilla. Pour into a strainer over a bowl to remove any lumps. Serve over ice cream, hot fresh made biscuits, or anything you like chocolate over.

Hot Cocoa Mix

1 ¾ cups nonfat dry milk powder
1 cup sifted powdered sugar
2 cups miniature marshmallows
⅓ cup unsweetened cocoa powder
½ cup powdered fat-free nondairy creamer

In a medium bowl combine dry milk powder, powdered sugar, nondairy creamer, and cocoa powder. Stir in the 2 cups marshmallows. Store in an airtight container at room temperature for up to 3 months.

For each serving, place 3 heaping Tbsp. of the cocoa mix in a cup. Add ¾ cup boiling water; stir well. Enjoy.

Marshmallows

2 Tbsp. & ½ tsp. unflavored gelatin
2 cups sugar
½ cup light corn syrup
½ cup hot water
¼ tsp. salt

2 large egg whites
½ tsp. pure vanilla extract
1 cup cornstarch
1 cup powdered sugar

Lightly spray a 9 x 13 inch glass baking dish with nonstick cooking spray. Sprinkle gelatin over a small bowl filled with ½ cup cold water; let stand to soften.

In a heavy bottomed saucepan mix together sugar, corn syrup, hot water, and salt. Place over medium heat and cook, stirring until sugar has dissolved. Continue cooking without stirring, until mixture reaches the soft-ball stage, about 240°F. on a candy thermometer. Remove from heat and add gelatin mixture; set aside.

In the bowl of an electric mixer, fitted with the whisk attachment, beat the egg whites on high speed until stiff peaks form. With the mixer running on low speed, slowly add sugar mixture. Add the vanilla then turn up the speed to high, and continue beating for 10 minutes until the mixture looks like marshmallow.

Transfer the marshmallow mixture to the prepared baking dish and spread evenly. Spray a piece of parchment paper with nonstick cook spray and cover marshmallow. Let stand overnight. Remove the parchment paper and invert marshmallow onto work surface. Cut into 2-inch squares.

Mix together the cornstarch and powdered sugar in a gallon sized zip-lock bag. Working with a few marshmallow squares at a time, cover them with powdered sugar mixture until all are done. Place them on a wire rack to dry for a couple of hours. Store in an air tight container.

Bread Pudding

About 10 slices white bread (day old and with crusts cut off)
6 Tbsp. softened butter
4 eggs
3 egg yolks
2 cups milk

1 cup heavy cream
⅔ cup sugar
3 tsp. vanilla
2 Tbsp. sugar
2 tsp. cinnamon
1 cup raisins

Preheat oven to 350°F.

Cut crusts off the bread and cut all but three slices in half diagonally. Butter all the slices. Mix the 2 Tbsp. sugar and cinnamon in a small bowl. Layer the buttered bread in an 8" round casserole dish, sprinkling the cinnamon sugar and the raisins after each layer.

Combine eggs and egg yolks in a large mixing bowl and beat until just blended.

In a saucepan combine the milk, cream, and sugar over medium high heat; bring to a simmer to dissolve the sugar. Slowly whisking constantly, add the hot milk to the eggs. Add the vanilla and pour over prepared bread and butter. Place the baking dish in a larger baking dish and place both in the oven, then pour about 1 inch of hot water into larger baking dish and bake for about 1 hour. Test with a knife until it comes out clean.

Serve hot or cold, plain, or with whipped cream or vanilla ice cream.

Serves about 8.

Bread Pudding - Chocolate variation:

To make this a chocolate bread pudding, increase the sugar to 1 cup and add ⅓ cup cocoa powder to the milk and cream mixture. Follow the recipe and use 1 ⅓ cups chocolate chips in between the layers of buttered bread and on the top of pudding.

Pots of Chocolate

1 cup chocolate morsels
1 egg
2 Tbsp. sugar
2 tsp. vanilla
Pinch of salt
⅔ cup boiling milk

In a blender add the first five ingredients and blend well. Add the boiling milk and blend again well. Pour into little cups or ramekins and chill for half an hour.

This dish is very rich!!!

Caramel

2 cups sugar
¾ cup light corn syrup
½ cup butter
1 cup whipping cream
1 cup whole milk
¼ tsp. salt

Bring sugar, corn syrup, butter, salt, and the cream to a boil, stirring frequently. Slowly add the cup of milk. Stir frequently as mixture thickens. Clip on a candy thermometer to the side of the pan. Stir the mixture until the thermometer reaches 255°F.

Pour into a buttered 8" square pan, and let cool for about 5 hours.

When cool, remove from pan and cut into squares with a sharp knife.

Lemon Curd

6 egg yolks, lightly beaten
1 cup sugar
½ cup fresh lemon juice
1 Tbsp. lemon zest
1 stick of butter, cut into pieces

Mix egg yolks, sugar, and lemon juice in a saucepan and cook on low heat, stirring constantly for about 10-12 minutes. Do not boil. Cook until it becomes thick and will coat the back of a spoon.

Remove from heat and add butter pieces and lemon zest. Mix until all the butter is melted and well mixed in. Pour into clean jars and refrigerate.

Makes about 1 cup.

Vanilla Custard Ice Cream

1 cup heavy cream
1 ½ cups milk
½ cup sugar
¼ tsp. kosher salt

1 whole vanilla bean
5 large egg yolks
2 tsp. vanilla extract

In a heavy saucepan stir together the cream, milk, half the sugar, and the salt. With a small knife split the vanilla bean in half lengthwise and scrape the seeds from the bean. Add the seeds and pods to the milk mixture and heat until the milk just bubbles around the side of the pan. Remove from the heat and cover. Let the milk mixture steep for about an hour. Remove the pods and discard.

Place the egg yolks in a medium size heatproof bowl and whisk just enough to break up the yolks. Whisk in remaining sugar until smooth. Set aside. Uncover the milk mixture and heat over medium heat until almost simmering. Using a ladle, carefully pour about ½ cup of hot cream mixture into yolks, whisking constantly. Repeat this several times. Stirring constantly with a wooden spoon, slowly pour yolk mixture into hot cream in the saucepan. Continue to cook on medium, stirring constantly in a figure eight to cover entire bottom of the pan. Cook until the mixture becomes the consistency of thick cream or a puree, but no thicker. If the mixture coats the back of a spoon then it is done.

Pour immediately into a fine mesh sieve over a large measuring cup and cover and refrigerate for 2 hours or over night, which is better. Stir in vanilla extract just before churning in the ice cream machine. Finish according to icecream maker directions.

Makes 8 servings.

Raspberry Curd

4 cups frozen raspberries
1 cup sugar
1 lemon, zested and juiced
3 egg yolks

3 Tbsp. cornstarch
⅛ tsp. salt
4 Tbsp. butter

In a saucepan, combine the raspberries, sugar and the lemon juice and cook over medium heat. Bring to a boil , then reduce heat to medium low and simmer for 6 minutes. Transfer mixture to the container of a blender and blend until smooth; do this in small batches. Strain through a fine-meshed strainer. Return the raspberry puree to the saucepan and heat on medium.

In a medium bowl whisk the egg yolks with the cornstarch and salt. Add about ½ cup of the hot raspberries to the egg mixture and whisk very well. Add the egg mixture to the remaining hot mixture whisking the whole time. Whisk and cook over medium until thickened, about 4 minutes. Remove pan from the heat and add the butter one Tbsp. at a time, whisking to combine. Refrigerate before using, at least two hours. Curd can be kept refrigerated for up to 1 week.

Makes about 2 cups.

Caramel Corn

½ cup corn syrup
1 cup butter
2 cups brown sugar
1 tsp. baking soda

1 tsp. vanilla
24 cups popped corn
2 cups peanuts

Preheat the oven to 250°F.

In a very large bowl put in the 24 cups of popped corn and the peanuts and set aside.

In a medium saucepan melt the butter and add the corn syrup and the brown sugar. Bring the butter mixture to a rolling boil for 5 minutes or 250°F on a candy thermometer. After it reaches the right temperature, turn off the heat and add the baking soda and the vanilla. Stir until it is completely mixed in. Pour the caramel onto the popped corn and mix very well, until every piece of corn is covered.

Pour the corn and caramel mixture into a very large roasting pan and put into the oven, set timer for 15 minutes. Take it out of the oven and mix it up. Return to the oven and do this again every 15 minutes for 1 hour. After the mixing is all done let cool completely and store in an air tight container.

Kristina's Rice Pudding

3 quarts whole milk
1 cup heavy cream
1 cup sugar
1 tsp. vanilla

1 ⅓ cup short grain rice
1 cup raisins (optional)
½ stick of butter

Bring the first four of these ingredients to a boil in a large pot. Then stir in rice, raisins (optional), and butter.

Simmer for 1 hour stirring often until pudding becomes thick and creamy.

Add 3 large eggs mixed with ¼ cup milk (blend eggs with milk in a blender.) Stir until egg mixture and pudding mixture are combined. Turn heat off.

You can half this recipe. It makes a lot.

This is Kristina's favorite, and instead of birthday cake she wants this pudding.

Chocolate Pudding

⅓ cup cocoa
½ cup sugar
3 Tbsp. Cornstarch

½ tsp. salt
3 cups milk
1 ½ tsp. vanilla

Mix cocoa with sugar, cornstarch, and salt; Gradually blend in milk. Cook over medium heat and stir constantly until mixture thickens. Cook for 2 or 3 minutes longer. Add vanilla and stir until blended in. Remove from heat and pour into 5 or 6 dessert cups. Chill until firm. Top with whipped cream and serve.

Canning

Pickled Peaches

1 cup white vinegar
3 ½ cups sugar
¾ tsp. whole cloves
¼ tsp. whole allspice
4 sticks whole cinnamon
4 pounds firm-ripe peaches or pears

Combine the spices in a cheese cloth bag and add to a saucepan with the vinegar and sugar. Heat until it comes to a boil. Turn off the heat and let stand for a few minutes.

Meanwhile, wash the peaches and cut in half, remove the pit, and remove the skin. Bring the vinegar mixture back to a boil. Add the peaches, cover, and simmer gently until the peaches are tender but not soft; about 2 minutes.

While waiting on simmering peaches, prepare the canning jars. Pack the peaches in the jars, with the cut side down and fill with the vinegar mixture to ¼ inch from the top of the jar. Put the jar lid and ring on and process in the water bath for 10 minutes.

Apple Pie Filling

6 pounds apples, peeled, cored, and sliced
4 ½ cups sugar
1 cup cornstarch
1 Tbsp. cinnamon
¼ tsp. nutmeg
2 tsp. salt
10 cups water
3 Tbsp. lemon juice

In a very large pan put all the ingredients in and mix very well. Place pan over medium heat and bring to a boil and cook and stir until thick and bubbly. Remove from the heat and pack into clean hot quart jars to within ¾ inch headspace. Wipe the rim with a clean wet cloth and seal with a lid and ring. Place in a water bath for 20 minutes. Remove from water bath and let cool to room temperature.

Makes 6 quarts.

Strawberry Syrup

3 pounds fresh strawberries (12 cups)
2 cups water
3 cups sugar

Wash and remove the green leaves. Put half of the berries in a large pot (6-8 quarts). Using a potato masher, crush the berries. Add the remaining berries and crush them. Add the water. Bring to a boil, reduce heat and simmer, uncovered, for about 5 minutes stirring occasionally.

Line a colander with a double layer of cheese cloth and place colander over a large bowl. Pour hot berries in the colander lined with cheese cloth and allow to drain. When the strawberries are cool enough to handle gather the four corners up and twist and squeeze out the remaining juice. Discard the pulp of the strawberries. Rinse the same pot and heat the strawberry juice to a rolling boil and add the sugar stirring until the juice comes back to a rolling boil, reduce heat to a simmer. Continue simmering uncovered for 20 to 30 minutes, or until the juice becomes the consistency of maple syrup. Stir frequently to prevent sticking.

Pour hot syrup into hot sterilized ½ pint jars leaving ¼ inch headspace. Wipe the jar rims and adjust the lids and screw bands. Process in a hot water bath for 5 minutes (start timing when the water returns to a rolling boil). Remove the jars from the canner and place on a clean towel to cool.

Makes about 4 half pints.

You'll be preparing the following syrups like the strawberry syrup, but with the exceptions listed under each type.

Blueberry Syrup

Use 6 cups fresh blueberries in place of the strawberries, increase the water to 4 cups, and boil with 4 Tbsp. fresh lemon juice. Cook the blueberries for only 25 minutes. Makes about 5 half pints.

Blackberry Syrup

Prepare the strawberry syrup as directed, except substitute with 12 cups fresh blackberries. 1 ½ cup water and 4 cups sugar.

Peach-Vanilla Syrup

Prepare strawberry syrup as directed, except substitute sliced, pealed, fresh peaches and reduce the sugar to 2 ½ cups. Cut one vanilla bean in half and scrape out the seeds, then set aside. Boil the vanilla pod with the peaches. Stir the vanilla seeds into the peach juice after straining. Makes about 5 ½ pint jars.

Raspberry Syrup

Prepare strawberry syrup as directed, except substitute fresh raspberries. Makes about 5 ½ pint jars.

Pomegranate Syrup

6 cups pomegranate juice
6 cups sugar
2 cups water
¼ cup lemon juice

Blend all the ingredients in a big pot and bring to a boil, reduce the boil to a simmer and simmer for 45 minutes, or until thick like maple syrup. With a funnel pour the hot syrup into hot 12 oz. bottles or ½ pint jars, put lids on and put into a hot water bath for 10 minutes.

Makes about 6 pint jars

Lemon Curd

12 lemons (juiced)
12 eggs, lightly beaten
2 Tbsp. lemon zest
1 cup butter, (2 sticks)
9 cups sugar

Wash and sterilize 14 eight ounce jars and lids.

Combine all the ingredients in a 6 quart heavy pan. Over medium high heat, and stirring constantly, bring the mixture to a simmer and reduce heat right away. Over low heat, simmer for 12 to 15 minutes until the mixture thickens and will sheet from a spoon. You should be able to draw your finger across the spoon and leave a line. Do not over cook, the mixture will thicken once you pour it into the jar and cools. Remove the pan from the heat and ladle the lemon into the jars, screw on the lids, and process in a hot water bath for 10 minutes. Start timing when the water comes to a roiling boil.

This amazing curd will last on the pantry shelf for about a year if not opened. Once you open a jar it needs to be refrigerated.

LaVon's Chili Sauce

15 large tomatoes
5 onions
1 bunch celery
5 bell peppers
3 Tbsp. salt

1 cup sugar
2 ½ cups cider vinegar
1 tsp. ground cinnamon
1 tsp. ground ginger
¼ tsp. ground allspice

In a food processor finely chop the vegetables.

Mix all the ingredients in a large pot and cook slowly for about 3 hours, stirring occasionally. Pour into sterilized canning jars with ring band lids, and put into a water bath for 15 minutes. Remove from bath and put on a clean towel to cool.

This recipe is good on meats and eggs.

LaVon is Richard's grandmother's cousin. When I got this recipe Nana, Richard's grandmother, was 94 years old.

Pickled Beets

20 medium sized beets
2 ½ cups water
2 ½ cups vinegar
1 cup sugar
2 tsp. salt
10 whole cloves
10 whole allspice
2 cinnamon sticks, broken

Clean the beets and cook until tender. Drain and remove the skins. Cut to the size you want and pack into your jars.

Combine the vinegar, water, and the sugar in a pan. Tie the spices in a cheesecloth bag and put in the pan of liquid and bring to a boil. Let steep for about 15 minutes. Remove the spice bag. Pour the hot liquid over the beets in the jars to within ½ inch of the rim.

Adjust the lids and process the jars in a hot water bath for 10 minutes.

Pickled Green Beans

2 lbs. fresh green beans
1 Tbsp. chili seeds
1 clove garlic for each jar

2 cups water
2 cups cider vinegar
½ cup coarse salt

Clean and cut green beans to fit the jars. Pack the beans in the jars stem end down. To each jar add 1 clove of garlic and ¼ tsp. of the chili seeds.

Combine the water, salt, and the vinegar in an enameled pan or a stainless steel pan and bring to a boil. Pour hot liquid over the beans, filling the jars to within ½ inch of the top. Wipe the rims; adjust the lids and tighten them.

Process the jars in a boiling water bath for 10 minutes. Start counting the processing time after the water has returned to a boil. Remove the jars and let cool.

They are ready to eat immediately, but are better when chilled.

Pomegranate Jelly

3 ½ cups of pomegranate juice
1 package of powdered pectin
¼ cup fresh lemon juice
4 ½ cups sugar

You can either:
1. Cut the crown end off each pomegranate and lightly score the peel lengthwise down the sides in several places, then hold the fruit under water and pop the seeds out.
2. Cut the pomegranates in half and juice them with an electric juicer.

If you pop the seeds out under water you are going to have to put the seeds in a blender and whirl them until liquefied. Pour through a cheesecloth lined wire strainer and let drain gradually.

Pour the pomegranate juice in a large pot, add the pectin and lemon juice, then bring to a boil. Boil for exactly one minute, add the sugar, and bring back to a boil for 2 minutes, stirring all the time. Pour into sterile half pint jars and seal with hot lids. I process the jars in a hot water bath for 10 minutes.

Makes about 6 one-half pint jars.

Apricot Jam

5 cups finely chopped apricots
½ cup fresh lemon juice
8 cups sugar

Discard pits, (do not peel), and finely chop apricots. Put apricots in a large pot and add one box of powered fruit pectin. Cook and stir fruit until it comes to a full rolling boil, stirring constantly. Stir in sugar quickly and return to a full rolling boil, and boil for exactly 4 minutes. Skim off any foam with a metal spoon. Pour cooked jam into prepared jars, seal, and put into a water bath for 10 minutes.

To make Apricot Pineapple Jam use 4 cups apricots and 1 cup crushed pineapple.

Own Mama, (AKA: Granny), would make the best apricot pineapple jam in the world. She is the one that taught me to make the jam, only she would peel the apricots. That is too much work, and I like the taste of the skins.

Blood Orange Marmalade

2 pounds, plus 4 additional blood oranges, cleaned & well and divided
2 cups water
3 Tbsp. fresh lemon juice
6 cups sugar, divided
1 box powdered pectin

Clean and sterilize 7 half pint jars, lids, and rings. Prepare boiling water bath canner.

Using a sharp knife, slice the top and bottom off of the 2 lbs. of oranges. Carefully remove only the rind, and cut into large strips leaving the white pith behind. In a medium saucepan put in the peels and just cover with cold water. Bring to a boil, and boil for 4 minutes then drain off water. Repeat this procedure two more times. When the peels are cooled and easy to touch slice into thin stripes. Remove and discard any of the white pith on the oranges and slice them into ½ inch thick slices.

Juice the remaining 4 oranges to make 1 cup juice. Combine the orange juice, orange slices, 2 cups water, orange rind, and the lemon juice in an enameled or stainless steel Dutch oven. Bring to a boil; reduce to medium-low heat. Simmer for about 45 minutes or until the peel is very tender. Add 5 cups of the sugar to the orange mixture and simmer for 30 minutes, stirring often. Stir in the pectin and bring back to a boil. Cook for 3 minutes. Stir in remaining 1 cup sugar and bring back to a boil. Cook another 2 minutes, or until the mixture reaches 220°F. on a candy thermometer.

Ladle the hot marmalade into the hot, sterilized jars and seal with the sterilized lids and rings. Process for 10 minutes in a boiling water bath canner.

Raspberry Orange Cranberry Sauce

1 bag cranberries (1 lb.)
1 cup raspberries
½ cup sugar

1 orange (zest removed and saved)
1 cup orange juice

Combine all the ingredients into a medium saucepan. Place over medium heat and bring to a boil, stirring to mix. Reduce to a simmer and cook until all the berries have popped. Cool and pour into a bowl with a cover. Refrigerate until ready to eat. This can be made up to a week in advance.

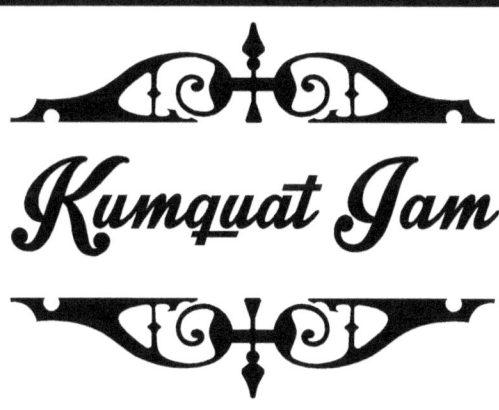

Kumquat Jam

3 cups kumquats, seeded and chopped
5 cups sugar
1 ½ cups water
¼ tsp. baking soda
1 box pectin powder

In a big pot put in the kumquats, water, and the baking soda and bring to a boil. Reduce the heat, cover, and simmer for 20 minutes, stirring occasionally. Stir in the pectin and bring back to the full rolling boil and boil for exactly one minute. Skim off the foam with a metal spoon. Add the sugar and stir until the full rolling boil returns, and let boil for one minute. Ladle into clean hot jars and seal with hot lids and rings. Put in a hot water bath canner and process for 10 minutes. Remove from canner onto clean towel and let cool until the lids make a popping sound.

Makes 10 ½ pint jars.

My dad has this big kumquat tree in the front yard and it seems wrong to let them all go to waste. So I make him marmalade every year, which he really enjoys. He used to make it himself, but now I do.

www.ingramcontent.com/pod-product-compliance
Lightning Source LLC
Chambersburg PA
CBHW042035100526
44587CB00030B/4434